10-27-01

Renee

Enjoy!

XOXO

RICE AND NOODLES

RICE AND NOODLES

OVER 75 DELICIOUS RECIPES FEATURING APPETIZERS, MAIN COURSES AND DESSERTS

EMMA LEE

LORENZ BOOKS

First published in 1999 by Lorenz Books

© 1999 Anness Publishing Limited

Lorenz Books is an imprint of
Anness Publishing Inc.
27 West 20th Street
New York, NY 10011
(800) 354-9657

ISBN 0 7548 0272 8

Publisher: Joanna Lorenz
Project Editors: Sarah Ainley and Emma Clegg
Designers: Patrick McLeavey, Jo Brewer & Partners and Ian Sandom
Jacket Design: DW Design
Illustrator: Anna Koska
Photographers: Karl Adamson, Edward Allwright, Steve Baxter, James Duncan, Michelle Garrett, Amanda Heywood and Thomas Odulate
Recipes: Carla Capalbo, Kit Chan, Jacqueline Clarke, Joanna Farrow, Rafi Fernandez, Shirley Gill, Shehzad Husain, Christine Ingram, Soheila Kimberley, Ruby Le Bois, Liz Trigg, Laura Washburn and Steven Wheeler
Production Controller: Don Campaniello

Previously published in two separate volumes,
The Little Rice Cookbook and *The Little Noodle Cookbook*

Printed and bound in Singapore

1 3 5 7 9 10 8 6 4 2

Contents

Introduction

Rice and noodles are classic and versatile ingredients. Traditionally they each form the basic element of a meal, and yet there are also innumerable creative ways of reinventing them in a variety of cooking styles, by combining them with other ingredients, spices and flavorings.

RICE

Rice is one of the world's oldest and most versatile foods. An excellent source of complex carbohydrates, it is high in fiber, provides useful amounts of B Group vitamins, and contains very little fat. The energy from rice is released slowly into the bloodstream, so it is not a quick-fix carbohydrate like sugar. Considering that it cooks quickly and easily, with little or no advance preparation, it can be used for an astonishing range of sweet and savory foods, and is easily digested. It is not difficult to see why this grain has continued to grow in popularity.

Rice grains are sourced from aquatic cereal grasses. Originally cultivated mainly in Asia, paddy fields (the word "paddy" refers to the plant that yields the rice) are now a feature of the landscape in Europe and America. Two-thirds of the world's people enjoy rice in some form every day, and new varieties are constantly being cultivated.

Rice is categorized in most cases as being either long- or short-grain. Long-grain varieties, such as Patna and basmati, tend to retain their shape and remain separate when cooked, whereas the stubbier short-grain types cook down to a creamy consistency that makes them the ideal choice for puddings or risottos. The grains of certain short-grain types tend to stick together when cooked, an attribute that makes them much sought after for sushi, croquettes or rice cakes. Some varieties, such as Thai rice, for example, have characteristics of both types. New varieties and blends appear constantly on our supermarket shelves, giving us every opportunity to expand our repertoire. Two recent arrivals are the red rices from California and the Camargue.

Rice, like pasta, combines perfectly with poultry, fish and shellfish (especially shrimp) as well as with vegetables. Vegetarians are amply—and imaginatively —provided for in these rice recipes, with dishes such as Parsnip, Eggplant & Cashew Biryani sharing the limelight with Broccoli Risotto Torte. Remember, too, that rice contains no gluten, so a dessert such as Thai Rice Cake is perfect for anyone on a gluten-free diet. Sweet suggestions using rice include a delight-ful recipe for Moroccan pudding, scented with orange flower water and spiced with cinnamon, and a sundae served with raspberries, nuts and chocolate sauce.

NOODLES

Noodles are the original fast food—simple, speedy and satisfying. Their history goes back thousands of years, to the time when man first learned to grind grain. After the discovery that flour could be used to bake bread, it was then a short step to discovering that when it was mixed with water and pressed or rolled into thin sheets, it could be dried and kept for cooking at a later date.

Long before Marco Polo made his much-vaunted voyages to the Far East, returning with recipes for ravioli and other specialties now almost exclusively associated with Italy, the art of noodle-making had been perfected in the countries of India, Japan, China, Malaysia and present-day Thailand. European cooks, far from sitting back waiting for an enterprising explorer to import this tasty type of food, were already adding bits of dough to soups and stews. The light and floury dumplings that resulted were known as "nudeln," giving us the word that has become so familiar today.

Asian noodles are made from a wide variety of grains, including buckwheat and rice, and are often enriched with egg. They may also be of vegetable origin. Cellophane noodles are made from mung beans, and soy beans, chickpeas, corn and even seaweed are just some of the sources of the hundreds of different varieties now available to us. Some types do not even need to be cooked, but are quite simply added to a pan of boiling water and left to stand while the cook swiftly stir-fries some crisp vegetables, and then adds a savory sauce.

Noodle shops are a familiar part of the street scene in many Asian cities. In

8

Bangkok, noodle kiosks cater to city workers' insatiable appetites, while the *klongs* (canals) are thronged with noodle barges. Noodle sellers visit the suburbs, too, trundling their wares on carts from house to house. The situation is similar in Vietnam and Korea, while in Japan there are elegant specialty restaurants offering steaming bowls of noodle soup, simply prepared noodles with dipping sauces and crystal-clear chilled noodle salads featuring beautifully carved vegetables. In many of these restaurants the noodle maker can be seen at work. Unlike his Italian counter-part, he does not roll and cut the dough, but shapes it into a short rope before twisting and whirling it through the air repeatedly to produce the long and slender strands.

As snacks and appetizers, noodles (and dishes made from noodle dough, such as filled wonton wrappers) come into their own. Spring rolls are one of the most convenient finger foods, providing the perfect way of using up small amounts of meat, fish or vegetables. Fried plain wonton wrappers make delicious chips for sandwiching simple stir-fried mixtures. Noodle soups, popular all over the world, can be either light and delicately flavored or served as hearty and satisfying main courses.

We've traveled the world to bring you this collection. Dishes range from rissoles to stir-fries and from paella to salads, and illustrate the versatility of refreshingly simple ingredients. Whether you enjoy a few spring rolls as a light snack, or sit down with the rest of the family to a hearty chicken and shrimp jambalaya, rice and noodles both provide endless ways of adding new interest to your menu.

9

Types of Rice

LONG-GRAIN WHITE RICE

Perhaps the most familiar type of rice in the West, this is used mainly for savory dishes. The rice is milled to remove the outer husk of the grain, then polished to remove the bran and give the white grains a sheen.

EASY-COOK RICE

Rice sold as "easy-cook" or "parboiled" has been treated with high pressure steam before being milled. The steam hardens the outside of the grain, so cooking takes a little longer, but the grains stay separate and are fluffy. Purists claim there is a loss of flavor because of the treatment process.

BASMATI RICE

The name of this rice means "fragrance" in Hindi, and aptly describes this delicately flavored long-grain variety. Basmati rice benefits from being thoroughly rinsed, then soaked for about 10 minutes in cold water, before use. It cooks more quickly than regular long-grain rice.

BROWN RICE

This is not a specific type of rice, but a term used to distinguish any grain that retains its bran coating. Also described as whole-grain rice, brown rice has a nutty flavor. Brown rice takes longer to cook than white; some cooks prefer to fry the grains for a minute or two before adding boiling water.

RISOTTO RICE

A collective name for several varieties of short-grain rice, all of which cook to a creamy consistency while retaining a bit of "bite." Arborio is the best known type of risotto rice. The secret of a good risotto is lots of patience. The hot liquid must be added gradually, with each ladleful being absorbed before the next is stirred in. The only exception to this rule is paella. Here the stock is added to the rice all at once, and the dish is allowed to simmer without being stirred.

THAI RICES

Thai jasmine and Thai fragrant rice are delicately scented long-grain varieties that have a characteristic stickiness when cooked. They cook very quickly and are best cooked with just one-and-a-quarter times the amount of water to rice. Salt is not usually added.

RED RICE

Rice grown in the wild is a light red color. New varieties, which are being bred to recreate this fabulous coloring, are now creating considerable interest. For red rice with a buckwheat flavor, try the semi-wild cultivar from the Camargue.

GLUTINOUS RICE

Also called "sticky rice," this term generally refers to a Chinese short-grain rice that sticks together on cooking. The name, however, is misleading, as the rice does not contain gluten. It is easy to pick up with chopsticks and can be easily shaped and rolled. Glutinous rice can be white or black and is often used for rice pudding, which can be served with sugar and coconut milk.

WILD RICE

Not a true rice, but an unrelated aquatic grass from Canada and North America. The long, dark brown grains are costly and take a long time to cook, but the nutty flavor is highly prized. A smaller grain, cultivated "wild rice" is cheaper and more widely available. It is often sold mixed with long-grain rice.

11

SUSHI RICE

As the name suggests, this sticky Japanese short-grain rice is used for making sushi.

Types of Noodle

CELLOPHANE NOODLES

Sometimes sold as transparent, or glass, noodles, these are clear and shiny. They are generally made from mung bean flour and must be soaked in hot water before cooking. Unlike some Asian noodles, cellophane noodles can be reheated successfully after cooking, and are a favorite ingredient in stir-fries.

EGG NOODLES

Available in skeins or bundles, egg noodles are widely used throughout Asia, and range from very thin strands to narrow ribbons. Both fresh and dried noodles are available, although the latter type is easier to come by. Egg noodles need little cooking; some varieties are simply added to boiling water, others need to be boiled briefly. Always follow the instructions on the package.

RICE NOODLES

Made from rice flour and water, these long dried noodle strands come in various thicknesses, ranging from very thin to wide ribbons and sheets, and are usually sold in neat bundles, tied with raffia. Fresh rice noodles are also available. Rinse rice noodles in warm water and drain before use. Rice noodles are traditionally served at Chinese birthday celebrations; the longer the strands, the more auspicious the omens for a long and healthy life.

RICE SHEETS

Square or round pieces of rice flour dough, these are used in much the same way as wonton wrappers, to provide a casing for a savory filling. The sheets are naturally stiff and must be softened before being rolled, either by brushing them with hot water, or by dipping them briefly in hot water.

RICE STICKS

The name is somewhat misleading; rice sticks are simply flat, ribbon-like rice noodles, sold in skeins. As with other rice noodles, they must be soaked in hot water and drained before use.

RICE VERMICELLI

Thin, white and brittle, rice vermicelli is sold in large bundles. When pre-soaked and drained, it cooks almost instantly in hot liquid. Small quantities can also be deep-fried straight from the package to make a crisp garnish for a soup or a sauce dish.

SOBA

These Japanese noodles are made from buckwheat (or a mixture of buckwheat and wheat flour) and are traditionally cooked in simmering water. Flavorful and quite chewy, they may be served either hot or cold, with a dipping sauce.

SOMEN

Wheat flour is used to make these delicate white noodles. Like vermicelli, they cook very quickly in boiling water. Somen noodles are sold in dried form, usually tied in bundles that are held together with a paper band.

UDON

Thick and starchy, these noodles are similar to Italian pasta, and can be substituted for linguine. Made from wheat flour and water, they are usually round in shape. A dried whole-wheat version is available at some health food stores. Udon are also sold fresh, in chilled vacuum packs, or pre-cooked.

WONTON WRAPPERS

It is perfectly possible to make your own wonton dough, but it needs to be rolled wafer-thin, and most cooks prefer to buy it as wonton wrappers — neat 3-inch squares, dusted with cornstarch. The wrappers can be frozen for up to six months. They thaw rapidly, and are then ready for filling and frying, steaming or boiling. Wonton wrappers can also be deep-fried, like chips, or used to make spring rolls.

13

Techniques for Rice

RINSING AND SOAKING

Basmati rice and wild rice both benefit from being rinsed in several changes of cold water, then soaked for about 10 minutes before being drained and cooked. The traditional way of rinsing the rice is to add it to a large bowl of water and swirl it gently with your fingers. Glutinous rice is also rinsed and then given a long soak.

COOKING IN AN OPEN PAN

Similar to the method for cooking pasta, this involves adding the rice to a large saucepan of lightly salted boiling water. When the mixture comes back to a boil, stir it once, then let the rice cook for 12–15 minutes (10 minutes for basmati or Thai rices). The grains will remain separate. After cooking, drain well, rinsing the rice in boiling water if desired. Let stand for 5 minutes before stirring.

COOKING BY ABSORPTION

Rinse the rice if necessary and put it in a saucepan. Add cold water to cover (amounts vary, so check package instructions, but as a general rule 1 generous cup of long-grain rice would require $2\frac{1}{2}$ cups) and add a little salt. Bring to a boil, stir once, then cover tightly and lower the heat so that the rice barely simmers. Cook basmati or Thai rice for 15 minutes other long-grain types for 20 minutes and easy-cook rice for slightly longer. Brown rice will need slightly more water and should be cooked for 25–35 minutes. After cooking, set the pan aside, still covered, for 5 minutes, then fluff up the grains and serve.

QUICK-START BROWN RICE

One way of cooking brown rice is to stir-fry the grains in a little butter before cooking them

in lightly salted boiling water. Use 1 tablespoon butter and 2½ cups water for every 1 cup of brown rice. Having added the water, bring it back to a boil. Stir and cover, then simmer for 35 minutes without lifting the lid. Stir the grains and serve.

REHEATING

Cooked rice can be kept in the refrigerator in a sealed container for 2–3 days. To reheat, place the rice in a colander, rinse with boiling water, then set the colander over a saucepan of boiling water. Cover the pan with a cloth and steam for about 15 minutes. To reheat in the microwave, place the rice in a serving dish, cover loosely and heat on High (100% power). Four servings require 2–3 minutes cooking time and the rice should be stirred halfway through.

FAST FLAVORINGS & QUICK TIPS

• Toss cooked rice with chopped fresh herbs just before serving.

• Fry sliced mushrooms in butter over high heat until they are tender and most of the liquid has evaporated. Toss into the rice.

• Cook brown rice by the quick-start method, adding a little curry powder when stir-frying the grains. Toss the cooked rice with toasted cashews or almonds or plumped golden raisins.

• Make a simple rice salad by dicing carrots and bell peppers of various colors finely and tossing them with freshly cooked and cooled rice. Add a simple vinaigrette.

• Use vegetable stock instead of water for cooking rice by the absorption method.

• Cook rice by the open pan method. Drain but do not rinse with boiling water. Pack the rice in well-greased molds, set in a warm place for 3–4 minutes, then invert onto individual plates. Holding the plate and the mold together, tap firmly on the work surface to release the rice. Lift the molds.

• Add bruised green cardamom pods and a cinnamon stick to rice pudding for an Asian flavor. Stir in rosewater just before serving.

15

Techniques for Noodles

STORING
Store dried noodles in the original packaging in airtight containers in a cool, dry place. They will stay fresh for many months. Fresh noodles (available in the chilled cabinets in Asian food stores) keep for several days in the fridge if sealed in the plastic bag in which they were bought. Check use-by dates. Fresh egg noodles and wonton wrappers can be frozen successfully.

If appropriate, they may be tossed with a little oil to prevent any strands from sticking together. At this stage they can be stored in an airtight container in the fridge for several days.

PREPARATION
Some noodles, notably cellophane noodles and rice noodles, must be soaked in hot water and drained before use. Follow the instructions in individual recipes. Noodles that are to be cooked twice (parboiled, then stir-fried or simmered in sauce) are initially cooked until they are barely tender, then drained, refreshed under cold running water, and drained again.

COOKING
Add noodles to a large saucepan of rapidly boiling, lightly salted water, and cook for the time recommended on the package. Unlike Italian pasta, which should retain a bit of bite, Asian noodles are cooked until they are tender. Avoid overcooking, however, which can make them soggy. Dried noodles are sometimes deep-fried for garnishing or for use as a noodle cake. In this case, do not pre-cook.

Preparing Additional Ingredients

MAKING TAMARIND WATER

Tamarind, the fruit of a tropical tree, is highly valued for its acidic flavor. Sold dry or as pulp, the fruit must be soaked in hot water before use. Mix about 1 tablespoon pulp with ¼ cup hot water in a bowl. Let sit for 10 minutes, then strain into a clean bowl, pressing the pulp against the sieve to make a thick liquid (tamarind water). Use sparingly.

PREPARING LEMONGRASS

Cut off and discard the dry leafy tops, leaving about 6 inches of stalk. Peel away any tough outer layers, then lay the lemongrass on a board and bruise it with the flat blade of a cleaver or heavy knife. Cut the lemongrass into thin slices, or chop it finely.

MAKING COCONUT MILK

To make 1 cup thick coconut milk (coconut cream), break ½ cup creamed coconut into chunks and place it in a heatproof bowl. Stir in ⅔ cup boiling water until the coconut is smooth and creamy. If the recipe calls for thin milk, soak ½ cup creamed coconut in 1 cup boiling water in a blender or food processor for 10 minutes. Process until smooth, then strain before use.

APPETIZERS, SNACKS AND LIGHT SUPPERS

Sushi

INGREDIENTS

TUNA SUSHI
3 sheets nori (paper-thin seaweed)
5 ounces very fresh tuna fillet, cut into thin strips
1 teaspoon wasabi (horseradish mustard), thinned
with water
6 young carrots, blanched
4 cups cooked sushi rice
SALMON SUSHI
4 eggs, lightly beaten
$\frac{1}{2}$ teaspoon salt
2 teaspoons sugar
5 sheets nori
4 cups cooked sushi rice
5 ounces very fresh salmon fillet, cut into thin strips
1 teaspoon wasabi, thinned with water
$\frac{1}{2}$ small cucumber, cut into 5 sticks

SERVES 10–12

1 Make the tuna sushi. Spread half a sheet of nori on a bamboo mat, lay strips of tuna lengthwise across and season with the thinned wasabi. Place a blanched carrot next to the tuna and roll tightly. Seal the roll with water.

2 Place a square of nonstick baking parchment on he bamboo mat and spread it with sushi rice. center the nori roll on top and wrap. Press to set, then cut into rounds. Make more tuna sushi in the same way.

3 Make the salmon sushi. Use the eggs, salt and sugar to make five simple flat omelets in a nonstick frying pan.

4 Place a sheet of nori on a bamboo mat, cover with an omelet and trim to size. Spread a layer of rice over the omelet, then lay strips of salmon across the width. Spread the salmon lightly with wasabi, then place a cucumber baton next to the salmon. Roll up firmly, then press the roll so that it forms an oval. Cut into slices. Make more salmon sushi in the same way.

Rice & Mozzarella Croquettes

INGREDIENTS

generous ½ cup long-grain rice, freshly boiled
2 eggs, lightly beaten
½ cup mozzarella cheese, grated
1 cup dried bread crumbs
oil, for deep-frying
salt and ground black pepper
fresh dill sprigs, to garnish
AÏOLI
1 egg yolk
few drops of lemon juice
1 large garlic clove, crushed
1 cup olive oil

MAKES ABOUT 16

1 Drain the cooked rice thoroughly. Cool slightly, then transfer to a bowl and stir in the eggs and grated mozzarella, with salt and pepper to taste.

2 Shape the mixture into 16 equal-size balls. Spread out the bread crumbs in a shallow dish, add the rice balls and shake the dish to coat them thoroughly. Press the crumbs on well and chill the croquettes for 20 minutes.

3 Meanwhile, make the aïoli. Put the egg yolk, lemon juice and garlic into a small, deep bowl. Add salt and pepper to taste. Gradually whisk in the oil, a  drop at a time at first, then in a steady stream, until the mixture is thick and glossy. Cover and chill.

4 Deep-fry the rice croquettes in batches in hot oil for 4–5 minutes or until crisp, reheating the oil as necessary. Drain on paper towels and keep hot. As soon as all the rice croquettes are cooked, garnish them with dill and serve with the aïoli.

Red Rice Rissoles

INGREDIENTS

2 tablespoons butter
2 tablespoons olive oil
1 large red onion, chopped
1 red bell pepper, seeded and chopped
2 garlic cloves, crushed
1 fresh red chile, finely chopped
generous 1 cup risotto rice
4 cups vegetable stock
4 drained sun-dried tomatoes in oil, chopped
2 tablespoons tomato paste
2 teaspoons chopped fresh oregano
3 tablespoons chopped fresh parsley
1¼ cups cheddar cheese,
cut into 12 pieces
1 egg, beaten
1 cup dried bread crumbs
oil, for deep-frying
salt and ground black pepper

SERVES 6

1 Melt the butter in the oil in a large saucepan and sauté the onion, pepper, garlic and chile for 5 minutes. Add the rice and stir-fry for 2 more minutes.

2 Pour in the vegetable stock and add the sun-dried tomatoes, tomato paste and chopped oregano. Season with salt and pepper to taste. Bring to a boil, stirring occasionally, then lower the heat, cover and let simmer for 20 minutes.

3 Transfer the mixture to a bowl and stir in the chopped parsley. Let cool, then chill until firm. When cold, shape the mixture into 12 even-size balls, using your hands. Press a nugget of cheese into the center of each rice ball.

4 Roll the rice balls in the beaten egg and then coat them in the bread crumbs. Place the rissoles on a plate and chill again in the refrigerator for about 30 minutes. Deep-fry the rissoles in batches in hot oil for 3–4 minutes, reheating the oil as necessary. Drain the rissoles on paper towels and keep hot. Serve with a side salad, if desired.

Stuffed Tomatoes & Bell Peppers

INGREDIENTS

2 ripe beefsteak tomatoes
1 green bell pepper
1 yellow or orange bell pepper
4 tablespoons olive oil, plus extra for drizzling
2 onions, chopped
2 garlic cloves, crushed
½ cup blanched almonds, chopped
scant ½ cup long-grain rice, boiled and drained
2 tablespoons chopped fresh mint
2 tablespoons chopped fresh parsley
3 tablespoons golden raisins
⅔ cup boiling water
3 tablespoons ground almonds
salt and ground black pepper
chopped mixed herbs, to garnish

SERVES 4

1 Preheat the oven to 375°F. Cut the tomatoes in half and scoop out the pulp and seeds with a teaspoon. Drain the shells upside-down on paper towels. Chop the tomato flesh roughly.

2 Cut the peppers in half through the stems. Scoop out the seeds. Arrange the peppers, hollows-up, on a baking sheet. Brush with 1 tablespoon of the oil and bake for 15 minutes. Transfer to a shallow ovenproof dish, add the tomato shells and season with salt and ground black pepper.

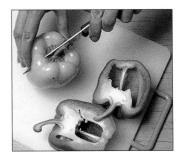

3 Heat the remaining oil in a frying pan and sauté the onions for 5 minutes, until golden. Stir in the garlic and chopped almonds and sauté over medium heat for 1 more minute.

4 Remove the pan from heat and stir in the rice, chopped tomatoes, mint, parsley and golden raisins. Season with salt and pepper and divide the mixture among the tomato and pepper shells.

5 Pour the boiling water around the stuffed vegetables. Bake, uncovered, for 20 minutes, then sprinkle the ground almonds on top of the tomatoes and peppers. Drizzle with a little extra olive oil. Bake for 20 more minutes, or until the shells are tender and the rice filling is turning golden. Garnish with the chopped mixed fresh herbs and serve immediately.

Stuffed Grape Leaves with Garlic Yogurt

INGREDIENTS

8-ounce package preserved grape leaves
1 onion, finely chopped
4 scallions, finely chopped
1/4 cup chopped fresh parsley
10 large mint sprigs, chopped
finely grated zest of 1 lemon
1/2 teaspoon crushed dried red chiles
1 1/2 teaspoons fennel seeds, crushed
scant 1 cup long-grain rice
1/2 cup olive oil
1 1/4 cups boiling water
2/3 cup plain yogurt
2 garlic cloves, crushed
salt
lemon wedges and mint leaves, to garnish
(optional)

SERVES 6

1 Rinse the grape leaves in plenty of cold water. Put into a bowl, cover with boiling water and soak for 10 minutes. Drain well, then dry on paper towels.

2 Mix the onion, scallions, parsley, mint, lemon zest, chiles, fennel seeds and rice in a bowl. Stir in 1 1/2 tablespoons of the olive oil. Season with salt and mix well.

3 Flatten a grape leaf, veins facing up, on a flat surface. Cut off any stalk. Place a heaping teaspoon of the rice mixture near the stalk end, fold the stalk end  over, fold in the sides, then roll up to make a cigar shape. Repeat to make about 28 stuffed leaves.

4 Place any remaining leaves in the bottom of a large heavy pan. Arrange the stuffed grape leaves on top in a single layer. Spoon on the remaining oil, then pour in the boiling water.

5 Invert a small plate over the stuffed grape leaves to keep them submerged in the water. Cover the pan and cook over very low heat for 45 minutes.

6 Meanwhile, combine the yogurt and garlic in a small bowl. Transfer the stuffed leaves to a serving plate. Garnish with lemon wedges and mint, if desired. Serve warm or cold, with the garlic yogurt.

26

Risotto-stuffed Eggplant

INGREDIENTS

4 small eggplant
7 tablespoons olive oil
1 small onion, chopped
scant 1 cup risotto rice
3 cups vegetable stock
1 tablespoon white wine vinegar
fresh basil sprigs, to garnish
TOPPING
⅓ cup grated Parmesan cheese
1 tablespoon pine nuts
SPICY TOMATO SAUCE
1¼ cups passata
(puréed tomatoes)
1 teaspoon curry paste
pinch of salt

SERVES 4

1 Preheat the oven to 400°F. Cut the eggplant in half lengthwise. Using a sharp knife, cut the flesh criss-cross fashion into neat cubes, then cut around the shells and ease the cubes out. Brush the shells with 2 tablespoons of the oil and place on a baking sheet. Bake for 15 minutes.

2 Heat the rest of the oil in a saucepan. Cook the eggplant cubes with the onion for 3–4 minutes, until softened. Stir in the rice and stock and simmer for 15 minutes. Add the vinegar.

3 Raise the oven temperature to 450°F. Spoon the rice mixture into the eggplant shells. Sprinkle the Parmesan and pine nuts on top. Bake for 5 minutes to brown the topping.

4 Meanwhile, make the sauce by heating the passata with the curry paste and salt in a small saucepan. Spoon the sauce onto four large plates, position two stuffed eggplant halves on each and garnish with basil sprigs. Serve immediately.

28

Spring Rolls

INGREDIENTS

6 Chinese dried mushrooms, soaked in hot
water for 30 minutes
1 cup lean ground pork
4 ounces raw shrimp, peeled, deveined and
chopped
4 ounces white crabmeat, picked over
1 carrot, shredded
2 ounces cellophane noodles, soaked in
hot water until soft
4 scallions, finely sliced
2 garlic cloves, finely chopped
2 tablespoons fish sauce
juice of 1 lime
4-inch rice sheets
oil for deep-frying
freshly ground black pepper
lettuce leaves, cucumber slices and
fresh cilantro leaves, to garnish

MAKES 25

1 Drain the mushrooms and squeeze dry. Remove the stems and slice the caps thinly into a bowl. Add the pork, seafood and carrot. Drain the noodles, snip them into short lengths and add to the bowl with the scallions and garlic. Stir in the fish sauce and lime juice. Season with pepper and set aside for 30 minutes to let the flavors blend.

2 Dip a rice sheet in a bowl of hot water to make it pliable, then lay it on a flat surface. Place about 2 inches of the filling near the edge of the rice sheet, fold both ends over, then roll up, sealing the roll with a little water.

3 Heat the oil to 350°F or until a cube of dried bread browns in 30–45 seconds. Add the rolls a few at a time and fry until golden brown and crisp. Drain

on paper towels and serve garnished with lettuce, cucumber and fresh cilantro.

Rice Vermicelli & Salad Rolls

INGREDIENTS

2 ounces rice vermicelli, soaked in hot water
until soft and drained
1 large carrot, shredded
1 tablespoon sugar
1–2 tablespoons fish sauce
8-inch round rice sheets
8 large lettuce leaves, trimmed
6 cups Chinese roast pork, sliced
2 cups bean sprouts
handful of fresh mint leaves
8 cooked jumbo shrimp, peeled, deveined
and halved
½ cucumber, cut into fine strips
fresh cilantro leaves
PEANUT SAUCE
1 tablespoon vegetable oil
3 garlic cloves, finely chopped
1–2 fresh red chilies, finely chopped
1 teaspoon tomato paste
½ cup water
1 tablespoon smooth peanut butter
2 tablespoons hoisin sauce
½ teaspoon sugar
juice of 1 lime
½ cup peanuts, ground

MAKES 8

30

1 Bring a saucepan of lightly salted water to a boil and cook the vermicelli for 2–3 minutes. Drain, rinse under cold water and drain again. In a bowl, mix the noodles, carrot, sugar and fish sauce.

2 Assemble the rolls one at a time. Dip a rice sheet in a bowl of hot water, then lay it flat. Place a lettuce leaf, 1–2 scoops of the noodle mixture, a few slices of pork, some of the bean sprouts and several mint leaves on the rice sheet.

3 Start rolling the rice sheet into a cylinder. When half the sheet has been rolled, fold both sides toward the center and lay 2 pieces of shrimp along the crease. Add a few cucumber strips and cilantro leaves, then finish rolling the sheet to make a tight package. Place on a plate and cover with a damp dish towel while you make the remaining rolls.

4 Make the peanut sauce. Heat the oil in a small saucepan and fry the garlic and chilies for 1 minute. Add the tomato paste and the water and bring to a boil, then stir in the peanut butter, hoisin sauce, sugar and lime juice. Lower the heat and simmer for 3–4 minutes. Spoon the sauce into a bowl, add the ground peanuts and let cool.

5 To serve, cut each roll in half horizontally to reveal the filling. Arrange on individual plates and add a spoonful of the peanut sauce to each. Garnish with any remaining cilantro leaves and bean sprouts.

Wonton Crisps with Seared Scallops

INGREDIENTS

16 scallops, halved
oil for deep-frying
8 wonton wrappers
3 tablespoons olive oil
1 large carrot, cut into long thin strips
1 large leek, cut into long thin strips
juice of 1 lemon
juice of ½ orange
2 scallions, finely sliced
2 tablespoons fresh cilantro leaves
salt and freshly ground black pepper
MARINADE
1 teaspoon Thai red curry paste
1 teaspoon grated fresh ginger
1 garlic clove, finely chopped
1 tablespoon soy sauce
1 tablespoon olive oil

SERVES 4

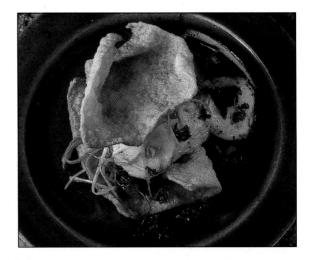

1 Make the marinade by mixing all the ingredients in a bowl. Add the scallops, toss to coat, then cover and marinate for 30 minutes. Meanwhile, heat the oil in a large heavy saucepan. Deep-fry the wonton wrappers in small batches until crisp and golden. Drain on paper towels and set aside.

2 Heat half the olive oil in a large frying pan. Add the scallops, with the marinade, and sear over high heat for about 1 minute, until golden and just firm to the touch. Using a slotted spoon, transfer the scallops to a plate.

3 Add the remaining olive oil to the pan. When hot, stir-fry the carrot and leek strips until crisp-tender. Season with salt and pepper and stir in the citrus juices.

4 Return the scallops to the pan, mix lightly and warm through. Transfer to a bowl and add the scallions and fresh cilantro. Sandwich a quarter of the mixture between each pair of wonton crisps. Serve immediately.

Chili Squid with Noodles

INGREDIENTS

1½ pounds fresh squid
2 tablespoons vegetable oil
3 slices fresh ginger, peeled and
finely shredded
2 garlic cloves, finely chopped
1 red onion, finely sliced
1 carrot, finely sliced
1 celery stalk, sliced diagonally
2 ounces sugar snap peas, trimmed
1 teaspoon sugar
1 tablespoon chili bean paste
½ teaspoon chili powder
3 ounces cellophane noodles, soaked in hot
water until soft
½ cup chicken stock
1 tablespoon soy sauce
1 tablespoon oyster sauce
1 teaspoon sesame oil
salt and freshly ground black pepper
fresh cilantro, to garnish

SERVES 4

1 Gently pull the squid's head and tentacles from its body. Discard the head; trim and reserve the tentacles. Remove the "quill" from inside the body and peel off the skin. Rub salt into the squid and wash in cold water. Cut the body into rings or squares.

2 Heat the oil in a flameproof casserole. Add the ginger, garlic and onion. Stir-fry for 1–2 minutes, then add the squid, carrot, celery and sugar snap peas. Stir-fry until the squid curls up. Stir in the sugar, chili bean paste and chili powder. Transfer the mixture to a bowl and set aside.

3 Drain the noodles. Combine the stock and sauces in the clean casserole. Bring to a boil, add the noodles and cook until tender. Add the squid mixture, cover and cook for 5–6 more minutes, until all the flavors are combined. Season to taste.

4 Serve on heated individual plates. Drizzle sesame oil over each portion and sprinkle with cilantro.

33

Sweet & Sour Wonton Wrappers

INGREDIENTS

16–20 wonton wrappers
oil for deep-frying
SAUCE
1 tablespoon vegetable oil
2 tablespoons light brown sugar
3 tablespoons rice vinegar
1 tablespoon light soy sauce
1 tablespoon ketchup
3–4 tablespoons chicken stock
1 tablespoon cornstarch, mixed to a paste
with a little water

SERVES 4

1 Make the sauce. Heat the oil in a wok or saucepan. Stir in the sugar, rice vinegar, soy sauce, ketchup and stock. Bring to a boil, then add the cornstarch paste, stirring constantly until the sauce is smooth and thick. Lower the heat so the sauce barely simmers while you cook the wontons.

2 Pinch the center of each wonton wrapper and twist it around to make the shape of a flower. Heat the oil in a wok or deep-fryer and fry the wonton wrap-pers for 1–2 minutes, until crisp. Remove with a slotted spoon and drain on paper towels.

3 Divide the deep-fried wontons between four plates and spoon a little sauce over each portion. Serve immediately, with extra sauce on the side.

34

Fried Cellophane Noodles

INGREDIENTS

6 ounces cellophane noodles, soaked in
hot water until soft
3 tablespoons vegetable oil
3 garlic cloves, finely chopped
4 ounces cooked shrimp, peeled and deveined
2 lap cheong or other spicy dried sausages,
rinsed, drained and finely diced
2 eggs
2 celery stalks, including leaves, diced
2 cups bean sprouts
4 ounces spinach leaves, torn into large pieces
2 scallions, chopped
1–2 tablespoons fish sauce
1 teaspoon sesame oil
1 tablespoon toasted sesame seeds, to garnish

SERVES 4

1 Drain the noodles, cut them into short lengths and set aside. Heat the vegetable oil in a wok, add the chopped garlic and fry until golden brown. Add the shrimp and lap cheong; stir-fry for 2–3 minutes. Stir in the noodles and fry for 2 more minutes.

2 Make a well in the center of the shrimp mixture, then break in the eggs and stir them gently over low heat until they are creamy and just set.

3 Add the celery, bean sprouts, spinach and scallions to the wok. Season with fish sauce and add the sesame oil. Toss over the heat until all the ingredients are crisp-tender, then transfer to a serving dish, sprinkle with sesame seeds and serve.

Egg Noodles in Soup

INGREDIENTS

8 ounces skinless, boneless chicken breast
or pork fillet
3–4 Chinese dried mushrooms, soaked in hot
water for 30 minutes
4 ounces canned sliced bamboo
shoots, drained
4 ounces young spinach leaves
2½ cups chicken stock
12 ounces dried egg noodles
2 tablespoons vegetable oil
2 scallions, thinly sliced
1 teaspoon salt
½ teaspoon light brown sugar
1 tablespoon soy sauce
2 teaspoons rice wine or dry sherry
few drops of sesame oil

SERVES 4

1 Using a cleaver or sharp knife, shred the meat finely. (If you put the meat in the freezer for 30 minutes before preparing it, it will be much easier to shred.) Drain the mushrooms and squeeze dry. Remove the stems and slice the caps thinly into a bowl. Shred the bamboo shoots and spinach leaves and add them to the bowl.

2 Bring the stock to a boil in a wok or saucepan. Fill a second pan with lightly salted water, bring it to a boil, then cook the egg noodles according to the instructions on the package. Drain, rinse under cold water and drain again. Transfer to a large serving bowl and pour in the hot stock. Keep the mixture hot.

3 Heat a wok and add the oil. When it is hot, stir-fry the chicken or pork with half the scallion for 1 minute. Add the mushroom mixture and stir-fry for 2 more minutes or until the meat is cooked.

4 Stir the salt, brown sugar and soy sauce into the wok, with the rice wine or sherry. Toss to mix, heat through for about 30 seconds, then drizzle with the sesame oil.

5 Add the stir-fried mixture to the noodle soup in individual serving bowls, garnish with the remaining scallions and serve.

Malay-Style Soupy Noodles

INGREDIENTS

1 tablespoon vegetable oil
2 garlic cloves, very finely chopped
2 shallots, chopped
3¾ cups chicken stock
8 ounces lean beef or pork, thinly sliced
5 ounces fish balls
4 raw jumbo shrimp, peeled and deveined
12 ounces egg noodles
4 ounces watercress
salt and freshly ground black pepper
GARNISH
2 cups bean sprouts
2 scallions, sliced
1 tablespoon fresh cilantro leaves
2 red chilies, seeded and chopped
2 tablespoons deep-fried onions

SERVES 4

1 Heat the oil in a large saucepan and fry the chopped garlic and shallots for 1 minute, then stir in the stock. Bring to a boil, then reduce the heat. Add the beef, fish balls and shrimp and simmer for 2 minutes.

2 Bring a large saucepan of water to a boil, add the noodles and cook until tender. Drain them well and divide among individual serving bowls.

3 Season the soup with salt and pepper, then add the watercress. The hot soup will cook it instantly.

4 Using a slotted spoon, scoop out the beef, fish balls, shrimp and the watercress from the soup and arrange them over the noodles. Pour the hot soup on top. Serve immediately, sprinkled with each of the garnishing ingredients.

Spicy Shrimp & Noodle Soup

INGREDIENTS

5 ounces dried rice noodles, soaked in hot
water until soft
¼ cup raw cashews
2-inch piece lemongrass, shredded
2 garlic cloves, crushed
1 onion, finely chopped
2 tablespoons vegetable oil
1 tablespoon fish sauce
1 tablespoon mild curry paste
1 can (14 ounces) coconut milk
½ chicken stock cube
1 pound white fish fillets, skinned and cut into
bite-size pieces
8 ounces raw shrimp, peeled and deveined
1 small head Romaine lettuce, shredded
2 cups bean sprouts
3 scallions, shredded
½ cucumber, cut into matchsticks
shrimp crackers, to serve

SERVES 4–6

1 Bring a saucepan of lightly salted water to a boil. Add the noodles and cook according to the instructions on the package. Drain, rinse under cold water and drain again. Using a mortar and pestle, or a food processor, grind the cashews to a paste with the lemongrass, garlic and onion.

2 Heat the oil in a large wok or saucepan, add the nut paste and fry for 1–2 minutes, until the paste begins to brown.

3 Stir in the fish sauce, curry paste and coconut milk. Crumble in the stock cube. Simmer for 10 minutes, then place the fish and shrimp in a large frying basket, immerse in the simmering liquid and cook for 3–4 minutes.

4 Line a large platter with the shredded lettuce. Arrange the bean sprouts, scallion, cucumber, fish, shrimp, noodles and shrimp crackers in separate piles on top. Ladle the soup into bowls and invite guests to add their own accompaniments.

Noodles with Ginger

INGREDIENTS

handful of fresh cilantro sprigs
8 ounces dried egg noodles
3 tablespoons peanut oil
2-inch piece fresh ginger, peeled
and cut into fine shreds
6–8 scallions, cut into shreds
2 tablespoons light soy sauce
salt and freshly ground black pepper

SERVES 4

40

1 Strip the leaves from the cilantro stalks. Pile the leaves on a cutting board and chop them quite coarsely with a cleaver or sharp kitchen knife.

2 Cook the noodles according to the instructions on the package. Drain, rinse under cold water and drain again. Transfer into a bowl and toss with 1 tablespoon of the oil.

3 Heat a wok, add the remaining oil and swirl it around. Stir-fry the ginger for a few seconds, then add the noodles and scallions. Stir-fry for 3–4 minutes, until the scallions are crisp-tender and the noodles are heated through.

4 Sprinkle the soy sauce and chopped fresh cilantro over the noodles. Add salt and pepper to taste and toss over the heat for about 30 more seconds. Serve immediately.

Chicken, Vermicelli & Egg Shred Soup

INGREDIENTS

3 large eggs
2 tablespoons chopped fresh cilantro
6 cups chicken stock
4 ounces vermicelli, broken into short lengths
4 ounces cooked chicken, sliced
salt and freshly ground black pepper

SERVES 4–6

1 Whisk the eggs in a small bowl and stir in the chopped cilantro. Heat a small non-stick frying pan and pour in 2–3 tablespoons of the mixture,  swirling to cover the bottom of the pan. Cook until set, then slide the omelet onto a board. Repeat until all the egg mixture is used up. Roll each omelet up. Using a sharp knife, slice thinly into shreds and set aside.

2 Bring the stock to a boil in a large saucepan. Add the vermicelli. Cook for 3–5 minutes, until almost tender, then add the chicken. Season with salt and black  pepper and cook for 2–3 minutes, until the chicken is heated through.

3 Stir in the egg shreds and serve immediately, in heated individual bowls.

Stir-fried Noodles with Spinach

INGREDIENTS

1 tablespoon sunflower oil
1-inch piece fresh ginger, grated
2 garlic cloves, crushed
3 tablespoons dark soy sauce
⅔ cup boiling water
2 cups peas, thawed if frozen
1 pound dried rice noodles
1 pound spinach leaves, coarse stalks removed
2 tablespoons smooth peanut butter
2 tablespoons tahini
⅔ cup milk
1 ripe avocado
roasted peanuts and peeled, cooked shrimp,
to garnish

SERVES 6

1 Heat a wok and add the oil. When the oil is hot, stir-fry the ginger and garlic for 30 seconds. Add 1 tablespoon of the soy sauce, then stir in the boiling water.

2 Add the peas and noodles to the wok, cook for 3 minutes, then add the spinach leaves. Toss over the heat for 1–2 more minutes, until the spinach is wilted and the noodles are tender, then drain the mixture and keep it hot.

3 Wipe out the wok and add the peanut butter, tahini and milk. Stir in the remaining 2 tablespoons soy sauce and mix well. Bring to a boil and simmer for 1 minute. Meanwhile, cut the avocado in half, remove the pit and peel and slice the flesh neatly.

4 Return the pea, noodle and spinach mixture to the wok, with the avocado slices. Toss gently to mix and heat through. Serve on individual plates, with some of the peanut and tahini sauce spooned over each portion. Garnish with roasted peanuts and peeled, cooked shrimp.

42

MEAT AND
POULTRY DISHES

Rice, Beef & Fava Bean Koftas

INGREDIENTS

generous ½ cup long-grain rice
1 pound lean ground beef
1 cup all-purpose flour
3 eggs, beaten
1 cup podded fava beans, thawed
if frozen, skinned
2 tablespoons chopped fresh dill
2 tablespoons butter
1 large onion, chopped
½ teaspoon ground turmeric
5 cups water
salt and ground black pepper
chopped fresh parsley, to garnish
naan, to serve

SERVES 4

46

1 Bring a saucepan of lightly salted water to a boil. Add the rice and parboil for 4 minutes, then drain thoroughly. Transfer to a bowl and add the ground beef, flour and eggs, with salt and pepper to taste. Knead until well blended.

2 Add the skinned fava beans and dill. Knead again until the mixture is firm and pasty. Shape into eight large balls, place on a plate and chill for 15 minutes.

3 Melt the butter in a large saucepan and sauté the onion for 3–4 minutes, until golden. Stir in the turmeric, cook for 30 seconds, then add the water. Bring to a boil.

4 Add the meat-balls to the pan. Lower the heat and simmer for 45–60 minutes, until the meatballs are fully cooked and the sauce has reduced to about  1 cup. Transfer the mixture to a serving dish, garnish with the parsley and serve with naan.

Thai Fried Rice with Pork

INGREDIENTS

3 tablespoons corn oil
1 onion, chopped
2–3 garlic cloves, chopped
4 ounces tender boneless pork, cubed
2 eggs, beaten
4 cups cooked rice
2 tablespoons fish sauce
1 tablespoon dark soy sauce
½ teaspoon sugar
GARNISH
4 scallions, finely sliced
2 fresh red chiles, sliced
1 lime, cut into wedges
1 small omelet, cut into strips

SERVES 4

1 Heat the oil in a wok or large frying pan. Stir-fry the onion with the garlic until softened, then add the pork and stir-fry until it is fully cooked.

2 Pour in the beaten eggs, stirring them into the pork mixture with a wooden spatula. Continue to stir over the heat until the eggs are scrambled.

3 Add the rice and stir gently to coat. Toss the mixture over the heat, taking care to prevent the rice from sticking to the pan.

4 Add the sauces and sugar. Mix well. When the rice is hot, transfer the mixture to warmed individual serving bowls. Garnish with the scallions, chiles  and lime wedges and arrange the strips of omelet on top. Serve immediately.

Turkish Lamb Pilaf

INGREDIENTS

3 tablespoons butter
1 large onion, finely chopped
1 pound lamb fillet, trimmed and cut into
small cubes
½ teaspoon ground cinnamon
2 tablespoons tomato paste
3 tablespoons chopped fresh parsley
½ cup dried apricots, halved
¾ cup pistachios, chopped
2¼ cups long-grain rice, rinsed
salt and ground black pepper
flat-leaf parsley, to garnish

SERVES 4

1 Heat the butter in a large heavy pan. Add the onion and cook until soft and golden. Move the onion to the side of the pan and add the lamb cubes. Brown on all sides, then sprinkle with the cinnamon and season with pepper. Stir, cover and cook gently for 10 minutes.

2 Add the tomato paste to the pan, then add enough water to cover the meat. Stir in the chopped fresh parsley. Bring to a boil, lower the heat, cover the pan and let simmer gently for 1½ hours or until the meat is tender.

3 Add enough water to the pan to make 2½ cups. Stir in the apricots, pistachios and rice. Bring to a boil, lower the heat, cover tightly and simmer for 20 minutes or until the rice is cooked and the liquid has been absorbed. Taste the pilaf and adjust the seasoning.

4 Spoon the pilaf into a warmed serving dish and garnish with the flat-leaf parsley. Serve immediately.

COOK'S TIP
It is important that the meat retain its tenderness.
Check the lamb occasionally while it is
cooking, and add more water if necessary.

Green Beans, Rice & Beef

INGREDIENTS

2 tablespoons butter
1 large onion, chopped
1 pound braising beef, cubed
2 garlic cloves, crushed
1 teaspoon each ground cinnamon, cumin
and turmeric
1 pound tomatoes, chopped
2 tablespoons tomato paste
1 1/2 cups water
12 ounces green beans, trimmed and halved
salt and ground black pepper
RICE
1 1/2 cups basmati rice, soaked
3 tablespoons butter
2–3 saffron threads, soaked in
1 tablespoon boiling water

SERVES 4

1 Melt the butter in a large heavy pan and fry the onion until golden. Move it aside and brown the beef cubes, then stir in the garlic, spices, tomatoes, tomato paste and water. Season with salt and pepper. Bring to a boil, lower the heat and simmer for 30 minutes, then add the beans and cook for 15 more minutes, until the meat is tender and most of the liquid has evaporated.

2 Cook the drained rice in lightly salted boiling water for 5 minutes. Lower the heat and simmer for 10 minutes, then drain, rinse under hot water and drain again.

3 Melt 1 tablespoon of the butter in the clean pan. Stir in a third of the rice. Spread about half the meat mixture on top. Continue to layer the mixtures until all are used, ending with rice. Melt the remaining butter and drizzle it on top. Cover tightly and steam for 30–45 minutes over low heat.

4 Spoon 3 tablespoons of the rice into a bowl and stir in the strained saffron liquid. Pile the remaining rice and beef mixture into a warmed serving dish, sprinkle the saffron rice on top and serve.

50

Chicken & Shrimp Jambalaya

INGREDIENTS

¼ cup lard
2 chickens, about 3–3½ pounds each, jointed
1 pound ham, rinded and diced
3 onions, finely sliced
½ cup all-purpose flour
2 14-ounce cans chopped tomatoes
2 green bell peppers, seeded and sliced
2–3 garlic cloves, crushed
2 teaspoons chopped fresh thyme
3 cups long-grain rice
5 cups water
2–3 dashes of Tabasco sauce
24 shrimp, peeled and deveined, tails left intact
6 scallions, finely chopped
3 tablespoons chopped fresh parsley
salt and ground black pepper

SERVES 8–10

1 Melt the lard in a large heavy pan. Fry the chicken pieces, ham and onions, turning occasionally, for 15–20 minutes, until the chicken is golden brown on all sides. Using a slotted spoon, transfer the mixture to a dish.

2 Lower the heat, sprinkle the flour into the fat remaining in the pan and cook, stirring constantly, until the mixture is pale golden. Stir in the chopped tomatoes, green peppers, garlic and thyme. Cook, stirring, until the mixture forms a thick sauce, then return the chicken mixture to the pan and cook for 10 minutes, stirring occasionally.

3 Stir in the rice, with salt and pepper to taste. Pour in the water, add the Tabasco and bring to a boil. Lower the heat, add the shrimp and cook until the shrimp are pink and the rice has absorbed the liquid. Both chicken and rice should be tender.

4 Stir in the scallions with 2 tablespoons of the chopped parsley. Spoon the jambalaya onto a heated serving platter, garnish with the remaining chopped parsley and serve immediately.

51

Yogurt Chicken & Rice

INGREDIENTS

3 tablespoons butter
3–3½-pound chicken
1 large onion, chopped
1 cup chicken stock
2 eggs
2 cups plain yogurt
2–3 saffron threads, soaked in
1 tablespoon boiling water
1 teaspoon ground cinnamon
2¼ cups basmati rice, soaked
½ cup zereshk or red currants
salt and ground black pepper
herb salad, to serve

SERVES 6

1 Melt 2 tablespoons of the butter in a large flameproof casserole. Add the chicken, with the chopped onion. Cook, turning the chicken frequently, until it is browned on all sides and the onion has softened.

2 Add the stock, with seasoning if needed. Bring to a boil, lower the heat and simmer for 45 minutes or until the chicken is cooked and the stock has reduced by half.

3 Drain the chicken, reserving the stock, and remove the skin and bones. Cut the flesh into large pieces and place in a large bowl.

4 Beat the eggs with the yogurt, strained saffron water and cinnamon. Add salt and pepper to taste. Pour over the chicken, stir to coat, then marinate for up to 2 hours.

5 Cook the drained rice in lightly salted boiling water for 5 minutes. Lower the heat and simmer for 10 minutes, then drain, rinse under hot water and drain again. Lift the chicken pieces out of the marinade and set them aside. Stir half the rice into the yogurt marinade.

6 Preheat the oven to 325°F. Grease a large ovenproof dish, about 4 inches deep. Spread the rice and yogurt mixture on the bottom, arrange the chicken pieces on top and then add the plain rice. Sprinkle with the berries.

7 Pour in the reserved chicken stock, dot with the remaining butter, cover tightly with aluminum foil and bake for 35–45 minutes.

8 Remove the dish from the oven and place on a cold, dampened dish towel for a few minutes. Run a knife around the inner rim, invert a platter on top of the dish and turn the rice "cake" out. Serve in wedges, with a herb salad.

Chicken Biryani

INGREDIENTS

2 tablespoons oil
1 onion, thinly sliced
2 garlic cloves, crushed
1 fresh green chile, finely chopped
1 tablespoon finely chopped fresh ginger root
1½ pounds chicken breasts, skinned,
boned and cubed
3 tablespoons curry paste
¼ teaspoon salt
¼ teaspoon garam masala
3 tomatoes, cut into thin wedges
1½ cups basmati rice, soaked
¼ teaspoon ground turmeric
2 bay leaves
4 green cardamom pods
4 cloves
6 cashews

SERVES 4

1 Preheat the oven to 375°F. Heat the oil in a large frying pan. Sauté the onion for 5–7 minutes, until lightly browned. Add the garlic, chile and ginger and cook for 2 more minutes. Add the chicken and stir-fry for 5 minutes.

2 Stir in the curry paste, salt and garam masala. Cook for 5 minutes. Add the tomatoes and cook for 3–4 more minutes. Remove from heat.

3 Bring a large saucepan of lightly salted water to a boil. Add the drained rice and the turmeric. Cook for 10 minutes or until the rice is almost tender. Drain, transfer to a bowl and toss with the bay leaves, cardamoms, cloves and cashews.

4 Layer the rice and chicken mixture in a shallow ovenproof dish, finishing with a layer of rice. Cover the dish with aluminum foil and bake for about 15 minutes or until the chicken is tender. Serve hot.

Chicken & Vermicelli Stir-fry

INGREDIENTS

½ cup vegetable oil
8 ounces dried rice vermicelli, broken into short lengths
5 ounces green beans, trimmed and cut in half lengthwise
1 onion, finely chopped
2 skinless, boneless chicken breasts, about 6 ounces each, cut into strips
1 teaspoon chili powder
8 ounces cooked shrimp, peeled and deveined
3 tablespoons dark soy sauce
3 tablespoons white wine vinegar
2 teaspoons superfine sugar
fresh cilantro sprigs, to garnish

SERVES 4

55

1 Heat a wok and add ¼ cup of the oil. When hot, add the vermicelli in batches and fry until crisp. Remove with a slotted spoon and keep hot.

2 Heat the remaining oil in the wok, then add the green beans, onion and chicken. Stir-fry for about 3 minutes, until the chicken is cooked, then sprinkle in the chili powder and toss over the heat for 1 more minute.

3 Add the shrimp, soy sauce, white wine vinegar and superfine sugar. Stir-fry for 2 minutes. Strew the fried vermicelli around the edges of four individual plates and pile a portion of the chicken mixture in the center of each. Garnish with fresh cilantro sprigs and serve immediately.

Noodles with Spicy Meatballs

INGREDIENTS

12 ounces dried egg noodles
3 tablespoons sunflower oil
1 onion, thinly sliced
2 garlic cloves, crushed
*2-inch piece fresh ginger root, peeled and cut
into thin matchsticks*
5 cups chicken stock
2 tablespoons dark soy sauce
2 celery stalks, thinly sliced, leaves reserved
*6 Chinese cabbage leaves, cut into
bite-size pieces*
*2 ounces snow peas, trimmed and cut
into strips*
SPICY MEATBALLS
2 cups ground beef
1 large onion, finely chopped
2 fresh red chiles, seeded and finely chopped
2 garlic cloves, crushed
1 tablespoon ground coriander
1 teaspoon ground cumin
2 teaspoons dark soy sauce
1 teaspoon dark brown sugar
juice of ½ lemon
salt and ground black pepper
beaten egg, for binding
oil, for shallow-frying

SERVES 6

1 Make the meatballs by putting all the ingredients except the oil in a large bowl and mixing thoroughly. Use only enough beaten egg to bind the mixture. Shape into small, evenly sized balls.

2 Bring a saucepan of lightly salted water to a boil and cook the noodles according to the instructions on the package. Drain, rinse under cold water and drain again.

3 Heat the oil in a large shallow pan and fry the onion, garlic and ginger until softened. Pour in the stock and soy sauce and bring to a boil.

4 Add the meatballs to the pan, then lower the heat and simmer, partially covered, for 5 minutes. Add the celery slices and simmer for 2 more minutes, then add the Chinese cabbage and snow peas. Simmer for 1 minute or until the meatballs are fully cooked.

5 Divide the noodles between six heated soup bowls. Add meatballs and vegetables to each bowl, then ladle stock on top. Garnish with the reserved celery leaves and serve.

Cellophane Noodles with Pork

INGREDIENTS

8 ounces pork fillet, trimmed and cut into very
small cubes
2 tablespoons dark soy sauce
2 tablespoons rice wine or dry sherry
2 garlic cloves, crushed
1 tablespoon grated fresh ginger
1 teaspoon chili oil
4 ounces cellophane noodles, soaked in hot water
until soft
4 Chinese dried mushrooms, soaked in hot
water for 30 minutes
3 tablespoons peanut oil
4–6 scallions, chopped
1 teaspooon cornstarch, mixed with
¾ cup chicken stock
2 tablespoons chopped fresh cilantro
salt and ground black pepper, to taste
fresh cilantro sprigs, to garnish

SERVES 3–4

1 Put the pork in a bowl with the soy sauce, rice
wine, garlic, ginger and chili oil. Mix well, then
cover and marinate for about 15 minutes.

2 Drain the noodles. Snip them into 5-inch
lengths. Drain the mushrooms and squeeze dry.
Remove the stems and chop the caps finely. Drain
the pork, reserving the marinade.

3 Heat a wok and add the oil. When hot, stir-fry
the pork and mushrooms for 3 minutes. Add the
scallions and toss over the heat for 1 more minute,
then stir in the cornstarch mixture with the
reserved marinade. Cook for 1 minute, stirring.

4 Add the noodles and stir-fry for 2 minutes, until
they have absorbed most of the liquid and the pork
is cooked. Stir in the chopped fresh cilantro, salt
and pepper. Serve garnished with cilantro sprigs.

Three-Meat Noodles

INGREDIENTS

1 pound dried egg noodles
1 skinless, boneless chicken breast
4 ounces pork fillet, trimmed
4 ounces lamb's liver
2 eggs
6 tablespoons vegetable oil
2 tablespoons butter
2 garlic cloves, crushed
4 ounces cooked shrimp, peeled and deveined
4 ounces young spinach leaves
2 celery stalks, thinly sliced
4 scallions, finely chopped
¼ cup chicken stock
dark soy sauce
salt and ground black pepper
deep-fried onions and celery leaves, to garnish

SERVES 6

59

1 Bring a saucepan of lightly salted water to a boil and cook the noodles. Drain, rinse under cold water and drain again.

2 Slice the chicken, pork and lamb's liver finely and set aside. Beat the eggs with salt and pepper to taste. Heat 1 teaspoon oil with the butter in a small frying pan. Stir in the eggs and cook over low heat, stirring constantly until scrambled. Set aside.

3 Heat a wok, then add the remaining oil. Stir-fry the chicken, pork and liver with the garlic for 2–3 minutes, until the liver has changed color. Add the shrimp, spinach, celery and scallions and toss over the heat for 2 minutes.

4 Add the drained noodles to the pan and toss again to mix. Moisten with the stock and add soy sauce to taste. Stir in the scrambled egg and serve, garnished with deep-fried onions and celery leaves.

Stir-fried Rice Noodles with Chicken & Shrimp

INGREDIENTS

8 ounces dried flat rice noodles, soaked
in hot water until soft
$\frac{1}{2}$ cup water
$\frac{1}{4}$ cup fish sauce
1 tablespoon sugar
1 tablespoon freshly squeezed lime juice
1 teaspoon paprika
pinch of cayenne pepper
3 tablespoons vegetable oil
2 garlic cloves, crushed
1 skinless, boneless chicken breast, thinly sliced
8 raw shrimp, peeled, deveined and cut
in half lengthwise
1 egg
$\frac{1}{2}$ cup roasted peanuts,
coarsely crushed
3 scallions, cut into short lengths
6 ounces bean sprouts
fresh cilantro leaves and lime wedges,
to garnish

SERVES 4

1 Drain the noodles, transfer them to a bowl and set aside. Mix the water, fish sauce, sugar, lime juice, paprika and cayenne in a small bowl.

2 Heat a wok, add the oil, then fry the garlic for 30 seconds. Add the chicken slices and shrimp and stir-fry for 3–4 minutes. Sweep the chicken mixture to the sides of the wok and add the egg to the center. Cook the egg, stirring it constantly, until it is lightly scrambled.

3 Add the drained noodles and the fish sauce mixture to the wok. Mix well, then add half the crushed, roasted peanuts. Toss over the heat until the noodles are soft and most of the liquid has been absorbed.

4 Add the scallions and two-thirds of the bean sprouts to the wok. Toss over the heat for 1 more minute, then spoon onto a large serving platter and sprinkle with the remaining peanuts and bean sprouts. Garnish with the fresh cilantro and lime wedges and serve.

Noodles with Beef & Black Bean Sauce

INGREDIENTS

1 tablespoon cornstarch
2 tablespoons soy sauce
2 tablespoons oyster sauce
1 tablespoon chili black bean sauce
½ cup vegetable stock
¼ cup vegetable oil
1 onion, thinly sliced
2 garlic cloves, crushed
2 slices of fresh ginger, peeled and finely chopped
8 ounces mixed bell peppers, seeded and sliced into strips
12 ounces round steak, finely sliced against the grain
3 tablespoons fermented black beans, rinsed in hot water, drained and chopped
1 pound fresh rice noodles, rinsed in hot water and drained
2 scallions, finely chopped, and 2 fresh red chilies, seeded and finely sliced, to garnish

SERVES 4

1 Put the cornstarch in a small bowl. Stir in the soy sauce, oyster sauce and chili black bean sauce, then add the stock and stir until smooth. Set aside.

2 Heat a wok and add half the oil. Stir-fry the onion, garlic, ginger and strips of mixed bell pepper for 3–5 minutes. Remove with a slotted spoon. Keep hot.

3 Heat the remaining oil in the wok. Stir-fry the steak with the fermented black beans over high heat for 5 minutes. Return the stir-fried vegetables to the wok, add the cornstarch mixture and cook, stirring, for 1 minute.

4 Add the noodles to the wok and toss over medium heat until cooked. Taste, and add more soy sauce, if necessary. Transfer the noodles to a heated bowl and serve, garnished with the chopped scallions and fresh chilies.

Pork Satay with Crisp Noodle Cake

INGREDIENTS

3 garlic cloves, crushed
1 tablespoon Thai curry powder
1 teaspoon ground cumin
1 teaspoon sugar
1 tablespoon fish sauce
6 tablespoons vegetable oil
1 pound lean pork, cut into 2-inch strips
12 ounces dried egg noodles, cooked, rinsed and drained
fresh cilantro leaves, to garnish
SATAY SAUCE
2 tablespoons vegetable oil
2 garlic cloves, finely chopped
1 small onion, finely chopped
½ teaspoon hot chili powder
1 teaspoon Thai curry powder
1 cup coconut milk
1 tablespoon fish sauce
2 tablespoons sugar
2 tablespoons lemon juice
½ cup peanut butter

SERVES 4

1 Mix the garlic, spices, sugar, fish sauce and 2 tablespoons vegetable oil in a bowl. Add the meat, toss to coat, then cover and marinate for at least 2 hours. Soak eight bamboo skewers in cold water.

2 Make the satay sauce. Heat the oil in a heavy saucepan and fry the garlic and onion for 1 minute. Stir in the spices and fry for 2 minutes. Add the remaining ingredients. Mix well. Cook over low heat for 20 minutes, stirring frequently, until the sauce thickens.

3 Heat 1 tablespoon of the remaining oil in a large frying pan. Spread the noodles in the pan and fry for 4–5 minutes, until crisp and golden. Turn the noodle cake over carefully and cook the other side. Keep hot. Preheat the broiler or light the barbecue.

4 Drain the meat and thread it neatly onto the drained skewers. Cook over medium coals or under the broiler for 8–10 minutes, turning occasionally and brushing the satays with oil. Transfer to a platter, garnish with fresh cilantro and serve with wedges of noodle cake and the satay sauce.

Noodle & Cabbage Rolls

INGREDIENTS

4 Chinese dried mushrooms, soaked in hot
water for 30 minutes
2 ounces cellophane noodles, soaked in hot water
until soft and drained
2 cups ground pork
4 scallions, finely chopped
2 garlic cloves, finely chopped
2 tablespoons fish sauce
12 large outer leaves of green cabbage
4 scallions
2 tablespoons vegetable oil
1 small onion, finely chopped
2 garlic cloves, crushed
1 can (14 ounces) chopped tomatoes
pinch of sugar
salt and ground black pepper

SERVES 4

1 Drain the mushrooms and squeeze dry. Remove the stems and chop the caps. Place them in a bowl. Snip the noodles into short lengths and add them to the bowl with the pork, scallions and garlic. Season with the fish sauce and mix well.

2 Cut out the stem from each cabbage leaf. Bring a pan of water to a boil and blanch the leaves and whole scallions for 1 minute. Refresh the vegetables under cold water and drain. Pat dry with paper towels. Split each scallion into ribbons by cutting through the bulb and tearing upward.

3 Place a spoonful of the pork filling in the center of each cabbage leaf. Roll up the leaf to make a neat package. Tie each roll with a scallion ribbon.

4 Heat the oil in a large frying pan and fry the onion and garlic over low heat for 5 minutes. Stir in the tomatoes, with salt, pepper and sugar to taste. Heat gently, then add the cabbage packages. Simmer, covered, for 20–25 minutes or until the cabbage rolls are fully cooked. Serve hot.

Braised Birthday Noodles

INGREDIENTS

2¼-pounds lean lamb shoulder, cut into
2-inch thick medallions
2 tablespoons vegetable oil
12 ounces dried thick egg noodles
1 tablespoon cornstarch
2 tablespoons soy sauce
1 tablespoon hoisin sauce
2 tablespoons rice wine or dry sherry
grated rind and juice of ½ orange
1 tablespoon red wine vinegar
1 teaspoon light brown sugar
4 ounces fine green beans, trimmed
and blanched
salt and ground black pepper
2 halved hard-cooked eggs and chopped
scallions, to garnish
MARINADE
2 garlic cloves, crushed
2 teaspoons grated fresh ginger
2 tablespoons soy sauce
2 tablespoons rice wine or dry sherry
1–2 dried red chilies
2 tablespoons vegetable oil

SERVES 4

1 Combine all the ingredients for the marinade in a large shallow dish. Add the lamb medallions, turn to coat, and marinate for at least 4 hours or overnight.

2 Heat the oil in a large heavy saucepan. Fry the lamb for 5 minutes, until it is browned, then add just enough water to cover. Bring to a boil, skim, then lower the heat and simmer for 40 minutes or until tender, adding more water if necessary.

3 Bring a large saucepan of lightly salted water to a boil. Add the noodles and cook for 1 minute only. Drain, rinse under cold water and drain again. Set aside.

4 Mix the cornstarch with the soy sauce and hoisin sauce, rice wine, orange rind and juice, vinegar and brown sugar. Add to the lamb and cook, stirring, until the sauce thickens.

5 Add the noodles and beans. Simmer, stirring occasionally, until both are fully cooked. Season and serve in individual bowls, garnished with the hard-cooked eggs and chopped scallions.

Fragrant Chicken Curry with Vermicelli

INGREDIENTS

1 chicken, about 3–3½ pounds
8 ounces sweet potatoes
¼ cup vegetable oil
1 onion, thinly sliced
3 garlic cloves, crushed
2–3 tablespoons Thai curry powder
1 teaspoon sugar
2 teaspoons fish sauce
1 lemongrass stalk, cut in half
2½ cups coconut milk
12 ounces rice vermicelli, soaked
in hot water until soft
lemon wedges, to serve
GARNISH
2 cups bean sprouts
2 scallions, sliced diagonally
2 fresh red chilies, sliced diagonally
8–10 fresh mint leaves

SERVES 4

1 Skin the chicken. Cut the flesh into small pieces and set it aside. Peel the sweet potatoes and cut them into chunks, about the same size as the pieces of chicken.

2 Heat half the vegetable oil in a heavy saucepan and fry the onion and garlic over low heat for 5 minutes. Push the onion and garlic to the side of the pan and stir-fry the chicken pieces until they change color.

3 Stir in the curry powder, cook for 1 minute, then add the sugar, fish sauce and lemongrass. Pour in the coconut milk and cook over low heat for about 15 minutes.

4 Meanwhile, heat the remaining oil in a large frying pan and fry the sweet potatoes until they turn pale gold. Using a slotted spoon, remove them from  the pan and add them to the chicken mixture. Cook for 15 more minutes, until both the chicken and the sweet potatoes are tender.

5 Drain the vermicelli. Bring a saucepan of lightly salted water to a boil and cook the vermicelli for 2–3 minutes, until tender. Drain, then divide between four individual shallow bowls and top with the chicken curry. Garnish with bean sprouts, scallions, chilies and mint leaves, and serve with lemon wedges.

FISH AND
SHELLFISH DISHES

Rice & Shrimp Casserole

INGREDIENTS

2 large onions, sliced and deep-fried
1¼ cups plain yogurt
2 tablespoons tomato paste
4 tablespoons green masala paste
2 tablespoons lemon juice
1 teaspoon cumin seeds
2-inch piece of cinnamon stick
4 green cardamom pods
1 pound jumbo shrimp, peeled and deveined
2 cups small button mushrooms
generous 1 cup thawed frozen peas
2¼ cups basmati rice, soaked
1¼ cups water
3–4 saffron threads, soaked in
6 tablespoons milk
2 tablespoons ghee (clarified butter)
salt

SERVES 4–6

1 Mix the onions, yogurt, tomato paste, masala, lemon juice, cumin seeds, cinnamon, cardamoms and a little salt in a bowl. Stir in the shrimp, mushrooms and peas. Mix well, cover and set aside in a cool place for 2 hours.

2 Grease the bottom of a heavy frying pan and add the shrimp mixture, with any juices. Drain the rice and spread it evenly on top.

3 Pour the water all over the surface of the rice. Using a spoon handle, make random holes through the rice. Strain the saffron milk and spoon a little into each hole. Dot with ghee.

4 Place a round of aluminum foil directly on top of the rice. Cover and cook over low heat for 45–50 minutes. Toss the mixture gently and serve immediately.

72

Lebanese Fish with Rice

INGREDIENTS

juice of 1 lemon
3 tablespoons corn oil
2 pounds cod steaks
4 large onions, chopped
1 teaspoon ground cumin
2–3 saffron threads, soaked in
1 tablespoon boiling water
4 cups fish stock
2¼ cups long-grain rice
⅔ cup pine nuts, lightly toasted
salt and ground black pepper
chopped fresh parsley, to garnish

SERVES 4–6

1 Mix the lemon juice with 1 tablespoon of the oil in a shallow dish. Add the fish steaks, turn to coat thoroughly, then cover and marinate for 30 minutes.

2 Heat the remaining oil in a large saucepan. Sauté the onions for 5–6 minutes, stirring occasionally. Drain the fish, reserving the marinade, and add the steaks to the pan. Fry for 1–2 minutes on each side, then add the cumin and a little salt and pepper.

3 Strain over the saffron water, then add the fish stock and reserved marinade. Bring to a boil, lower the heat and simmer for 8–10 minutes, until the fish is almost cooked.

4 Using a slotted spoon, transfer the fish steaks to a platter. Add the rice to the stock. Bring to a boil, lower the heat and simmer for 15 minutes.

5 Arrange the fish steaks on top of the rice. Cover tightly and steam for 15–20 minutes over low heat. Transfer the fish to a plate, then spoon the rice onto a large flat platter. Arrange the fish on top, sprinkle with the pine nuts and garnish with the chopped fresh parsley. Serve immediately.

Smoked Fish Kedgeree

INGREDIENTS

1 pound mixed smoked fish
1¼ cups milk
scant 1 cup long-grain rice
1 lemon slice
¼ cup butter
1 onion, finely chopped
2 teaspoons garam masala
½ teaspoon grated nutmeg
1 tablespoon chopped fresh parsley
salt and ground black pepper
fresh flat-leaf parsley and 2 hard-boiled eggs, halved, to serve

SERVES 6

1 Poach the un-cooked smoked fish in the milk for 10 minutes, until it flakes when test-ed with the tip of a knife. Drain, dis-carding the milk, and flake the fish.

Place it in a bowl and add any smoked fish that does not require cooking.

2 Then bring a saucepan of lightly salted water to a boil. Add the rice and the lemon slice and cook for 12 minutes, until the rice is just ten-der. Drain well.

3 Melt the butter in a large heavy saucepan. Add the chopped onion and cook until softened, then stir in the rice and fish. Shake the pan to mix the ingredi-ents thoroughly. Toss over the heat for 2 minutes.

4 Stir in the garam masala, grated nutmeg and parsley, and add salt and pepper to taste. Transfer the mixture to a warmed dish, garnish with the flat-leaf parsley and the hard-boiled eggs and serve immediately.

74

Seafood Risotto

INGREDIENTS

¼ cup sunflower oil
1 onion, chopped
2 garlic cloves, crushed
generous 1 cup risotto rice
7 tablespoons white wine
6 cups hot fish stock
12 ounces mixed seafood (shrimp,
mussels, squid rings, clams)
grated zest of ½ lemon
2 tablespoons tomato paste
1 tablespoon chopped fresh parsley
salt and ground black pepper

SERVES 4

1 Heat the oil in a large heavy saucepan and gently cook the onion and garlic for 4–5 minutes, until soft. Add the rice and stir into the contents of the pan to coat the grains with oil. Pour in the white wine and stir over medium heat for 2–3 minutes, until it has been absorbed.

2 Add ⅔ cup of the hot stock. Cook, stirring constantly, until it has been absorbed. Stir in a similar amount of stock until it has been absorbed. Continue in this way until you have added about half the stock.

3 Stir in the mixed seafood and cook over medium heat for 2–3 minutes. Add the remaining half of the stock as before, until the rice is creamy and tender.

4 Stir in the lemon zest, tomato paste and the chopped fresh parsley. Season with plenty of salt and ground black pepper. The risotto should be served warm rather than piping hot.

COOK'S TIP
Heat the fish stock in a saucepan before you start preparing the risotto, and keep it at a low simmer. Adding it in small amounts while stirring is the secret of a smooth, creamy dish.

New Orleans Bacon & Seafood Rice

INGREDIENTS

2 tablespoons corn oil
4 ounces bacon, diced
1 onion, chopped
2 celery stalks, chopped
2 large garlic cloves, chopped
1 teaspoon cayenne pepper
2 bay leaves
1 teaspoon dried oregano
2½ teaspoons dried thyme
4 tomatoes, peeled and chopped
⅔ cup passata (puréed tomatoes)
1¾ cups long-grain rice
2 cups stock
6 ounces skinned haddock fillets, cubed
4 ounces cooked, peeled shrimp
salt and ground black pepper
2 scallions, chopped, to garnish

SERVES 4

1 Preheat the oven to 350°F. Heat the oil in a flameproof casserole and fry the bacon until crisp. Add the chopped onion and celery and stir until soft and golden brown.

2 Add the chopped garlic, cayenne, dried herbs and chopped tomatoes, with salt and pepper to taste. Stir in the passata, rice and stock. Bring to a boil.

3 Stir the fish cubes into the rice mixture. Cover tightly. Put the casserole in the oven and bake for 20–30 minutes, until the rice is just tender.

4 Stir in the shrimp and heat through. Sprinkle with the chopped scallions and serve immediately.

COOK'S TIP
For a special-occasion garnish, add a whole cooked shrimp, in the shell, and a scallion tassel, to each portion.

78

Spanish Seafood Paella

INGREDIENTS

4 tablespoons olive oil
8 ounces monkfish, skinned and cubed
3 prepared baby squid, body cut into rings and
tentacles chopped
1 onion, chopped
3 garlic cloves, finely chopped
1 red bell pepper, seeded and sliced
4 tomatoes, peeled and chopped
generous 1 cup risotto rice
1¾ cups fish stock
⅔ cup white wine
4–5 saffron threads, soaked in
2 tablespoons boiling water
¾ cup frozen peas
4 ounces cooked, peeled shrimps
8 fresh mussels, scrubbed and debearded
salt and ground black pepper
chopped fresh parsley, to garnish
lemon wedges, to serve

SERVES 4

80

1 Heat 2 tablespoons of the oil in a paella pan and stir-fry the monkfish cubes with the squid for 2 minutes. Transfer to a bowl and set aside.

2 Heat the remaining oil in the clean pan and sauté the onion, garlic and pepper until softened. Stir in the tomatoes and rice. Cook for 4 minutes, stirring, then add the fish stock, wine, strained saffron liquid and peas, with salt and pepper to taste.

3 Gently stir in the monkfish, squid and shrimp. Push the mussels into the rice. Cover tightly. Cook gently for 30 minutes, until most of the stock has been absorbed and the mussels have opened. (Discard any that remain closed.)

4 Remove the paella from heat. Let stand, covered, for 5 minutes. Sprinkle with the parsley and serve with lemon wedges.

Fried Singapore Noodles

INGREDIENTS

6 ounces dried rice noodles, soaked in hot water
until soft
¼ cup vegetable oil
½ teaspoon salt
½ teaspoon sugar
2 teaspoons curry powder
3 ounces cooked shrimp, peeled and deveined
6 ounces cold roast pork, cut into matchsticks
1 green bell pepper, seeded and chopped
into matchsticks
3 ounces Thai fish cakes (optional)
2 teaspoons dark soy sauce

SERVES 4

1 Drain the noodles. Pat them dry with paper towels. Heat a wok, then add half the oil. When hot, add the noodles and salt. Toss over the heat for 2 minutes, then  use two slotted spoons to drain the noodles and transfer them to a serving dish. Keep hot.

2 Gently heat the remaining oil in the wok. Stir in the sugar and curry powder and fry for 30 seconds. Add the shrimp, pork and pepper. Stir-fry for 1 minute.

3 Return the noodles to the wok and add the Thai fish cakes, if you are using them. Stir-fry for 2 more minutes, until heated through. Stir in the soy sauce and serve immediately.

Stir-fried Noodles with Salmon

INGREDIENTS

12 ounces salmon fillet
3 garlic cloves
2 tablespoons Japanese soy sauce (shoyu)
2 tablespoons sake
¼ cup mirin or sweet sherry
1 teaspoon light brown sugar
2 teaspoons grated fresh root ginger
2 tablespoons peanut oil
*8 ounces dried egg noodles, cooked
and drained*
1 cup alfalfa sprouts
*2 tablespoons sesame seeds, lightly toasted,
to garnish*

SERVES 4

82

1 Slice the salmon thinly and spread the slices out in a large shallow dish. Crush 1 garlic clove and slice the remaining garlic thinly. Mix the soy sauce, sake, mirin, 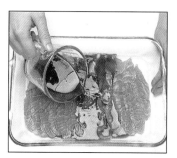 sugar, ginger and crushed garlic in a bowl. Pour the mixture over the salmon slices, cover and marinate for 30 minutes.

2 Carefully drain the salmon slices, reserving the marinade. Scrape any remaining pieces of ginger or garlic off the fish, then arrange the salmon slices in a  single layer in a large casserole dish and set aside. Preheat the broiler.

3 Heat a wok, add the oil and swirl it around. Cook the sliced garlic until it is golden brown, then add the cooked noodles and reserved marinade. Stir-fry for  3–4 minutes, until the marinade has reduced to a syrupy glaze that coats the noodles.

4 Meanwhile, cook the salmon slices under the hot broiler for 2–3 minutes without turning. When the salmon is tender, toss the alfalfa sprouts with the noodle mixture and arrange on four individual heated plates. Top the noodle mixture with the salmon slices and sprinkle the toasted sesame seeds on top. Serve immediately.

Seafood Chow Mein

INGREDIENTS

3 ounces squid, cleaned (see Chili Squid
with Noodles)
½ egg white
1 tablespoon cornstarch, mixed to a
paste with water
3 ounces raw shrimp, peeled, deveined and
cut in half lengthwise
3–4 fresh scallops, each cut into 3–4 slices
9 ounces dried egg noodles
5–6 tablespoons vegetable oil
2 ounces snow peas, trimmed
½ teaspoon salt
½ teaspoon light brown sugar
1 tablespoon rice wine or dry sherry
2 tablespoons soy sauce
2 scallions, finely sliced
vegetable stock to moisten (optional)
few drops of sesame oil

SERVES 4

84

1 Open up the body of the squid and score the inner flesh in a criss-cross pattern. Cut it into tiny pieces, each about the size of a stamp. Add them to a bowl of boiling water and set aside until all of them have curled up. Rinse under cold water and drain.

2 Whisk the egg white and cornstarch paste in a bowl, add the shrimp and scallops and stir to coat. Bring a saucepan of lightly salted water to a boil and cook the noodles. Drain, rinse under cold water and drain again. Transfer into a bowl and toss with 1 tablespoon of the oil.

3 Heat 2–3 tablespoons oil in a wok. Stir-fry the snow peas and seafood for 2 minutes. Add the salt, sugar and the wine, then stir in half the soy sauce. Add half the scallions and moisten with a little stock if necessary. Toss over the heat for 1 minute, then remove and keep hot.

4 Heat the remaining oil in the wok. Stir-fry the noodles with the remaining soy sauce for 2–3 minutes. Place in a serving dish and mix in the seafood mixture. Garnish with the remaining scallions and drizzle with the sesame oil. Serve hot or cold.

Lemongrass Shrimp

INGREDIENTS

*11 ounces thin dried egg noodles, cooked
and drained*
¼ cup vegetable oil
*1¼ pounds raw jumbo shrimp, peeled
and deveined*
½ teaspoon ground coriander
1 tablespoon ground turmeric
2 garlic cloves, finely chopped
*2 slices of fresh ginger, peeled and
finely chopped*
2 lemongrass stalks, finely chopped
2 shallots, finely chopped
1 tablespoon tomato paste
1 cup coconut cream
1–2 tablespoons fresh lime juice
1–2 tablespoons fish sauce
*1 cucumber, peeled, seeded and cut into
2-inch batons*
1 tomato, peeled, seeded and cut into strips
2 fresh red chilies, seeded and thinly sliced
salt and ground black pepper
scallions and fresh cilantro, to garnish

SERVES 4

1 Fry the noodles in 1 tablespoon of the oil as described for Pork Satay with Crisp Noodle Cake (page 55), to make four individual cakes. Keep hot.

2 Put the shrimp, ground spices, garlic, ginger and lemongrass in a bowl. Add salt and pepper to taste and toss to coat. Heat the remaining oil in a large frying pan and stir-fry the shallots for 1 minute, then add the seasoned shrimp and stir-fry for 2 minutes. Remove the shrimp with a slotted spoon.

3 Stir the tomato paste and coconut cream into the mixture remaining in the pan. Add lime juice and fish sauce to taste. Bring to the simmering point, then add the cucumber. Return the shrimp to the sauce and simmer for 3–4 minutes, until they are tender and the sauce is thick.

4 Add the tomato, stir until heated, then add the chilies. Serve on the noodle cakes, garnished with sliced scallions and fresh cilantro sprigs.

Spicy Fried Rice Sticks

INGREDIENTS

*½ ounce dried shrimps, soaked in hot water for
30 minutes*
*8 ounces dried rice sticks, soaked in hot water
for 30 minutes*
2 tablespoons tamarind water
3 tablespoons fish sauce
1 tablespoon sugar
2 garlic cloves, chopped
2 fresh red chilies, seeded and chopped
3 tablespoons peanut oil
2 eggs, beaten
*8 ounces cooked jumbo shrimp, peeled
and deveined*
3 scallions, cut into 1-inch lengths
1½ cups bean sprouts
2 tablespoons chopped roasted unsalted peanuts
2 tablespoons chopped fresh cilantro
lime slices, to garnish

SERVES 4

1 Drain the shrimps and set them aside. Drain the
rice sticks, rinse them under cold running water
and drain again. Mix the tamarind water with the
fish sauce and sugar.

2 Put the garlic and chilies in a mortar and use a
pestle to pound them to a paste. Heat a wok, add
1 tablespoon of the oil, then stir-fry the eggs over
medium heat until lightly scrambled. Transfer the
eggs to a bowl and set aside. Wipe the wok clean.

3 Reheat the wok, add the remaining oil, then fry
the chili and garlic paste with the dried shrimps for
1 minute. Add the rice sticks and tamarind mixture;
toss over the heat for 3–4 minutes.

4 Add the scrambled eggs, shrimp, scallions, bean
sprouts, peanuts and cilantro to the wok. Toss over
the heat for 2 minutes, until heated through and
well mixed. Serve immediately on individual plates,
garnishing each portion with lime slices.

COOK'S TIP

*For a vegetarian dish, leave out the dried
shrimps and use cubes of deep-fried, plain
or smoked, firm tofu instead of the shrimp.*

VEGETABLES,
VEGETARIAN DISHES
AND SALADS

Broccoli Risotto Torte

Ingredients

8oz broccoli, cut into tiny florets
¼ cup butter
2 tablespoons olive oil, plus extra for greasing
1 onion, chopped
2 garlic cloves, crushed
1 large yellow bell pepper, seeded and sliced
generous 1 cup risotto rice
½ cup dry white wine
4 cups vegetable stock
1⅓ cups grated Parmesan cheese
4 eggs, separated
salt and ground black pepper
tomato slices and chopped parsley, to garnish

Serves 4

1 Blanch the broccoli in boiling water for 3 minutes, drain and set aside. Melt the butter in the oil in a frying pan. Sauté the onion, garlic and pepper until soft.

2 Stir in the rice, cook for 1 minute, then pour in the wine. Cook, stirring constantly, until it is absorbed. Pour in the stock and season well. Bring to a boil, lower the heat and simmer for 20 minutes, stirring occasionally.

3 Preheat the oven to 350°F. Lightly grease a deep 10-inch round cake pan and line the bottom with nonstick baking parchment. Stir the cheese into the rice mixture, cool for 5 minutes, then beat in the egg yolks. Fold in the broccoli.

4 Whisk the egg whites to stiff peaks; fold them into the rice. Spoon into the prepared pan and bake for 1 hour, until risen, golden and still slightly soft in the center. Cool slightly, then invert on a serving plate, peel off the paper and turn back onto another serving plate. Garnish with tomato slices and parsley. This torte is also good served cold.

Risotto alla Milanese

INGREDIENTS

2 tablespoons butter
1 large onion, finely chopped
1½ cups risotto rice
⅔ cup dry white wine
1 teaspoon saffron threads soaked in
1 tablespoon boiling water
4 cups vegetable stock
salt and ground black pepper
Parmesan cheese shavings, to garnish
GREMOLATA
2 garlic cloves, crushed
¼ cup chopped fresh parsley
finely grated zest of 1 lemon

SERVES 4

1 Make the gremolata by mixing the garlic and parsley in a bowl. Stir in the grated lemon zest and set aside.

2 Melt the butter in a heavy saucepan. Add the onion and sauté over low heat for 5 minutes. Stir in the rice until well coated. Cook for 2 minutes, until it is translucent, then add the wine and strain in the saffron liquid. Cook for 3–4 minutes, until the liquid has been absorbed.

3 Add 2½ cups of the stock to the saucepan. Simmer, stirring frequently, until it has been absorbed. Gradually add the remaining stock, a ladleful at a time, until the rice is tender and creamy. Let each quantity of stock be absorbed before adding the next (it may not be necessary to add it all).

91

4 Season the risotto with plenty of salt and pepper. Transfer it to a serving dish. Sprinkle lavishly with the Parmesan shavings and gremolata on top. Serve hot.

Mexican-style Rice

INGREDIENTS

1¾ cups long-grain white rice
1 onion, chopped
2 garlic cloves, chopped
1 pound tomatoes, peeled, seeded and
coarsely chopped
¼ cup corn or peanut oil
3¾ cups chicken stock
4–6 small red chiles
1 cup cooked green peas
salt and ground black pepper
coriander springs, to garnish

SERVES 6

92

1 First, soak the rice in a bowl of hot water for 15 minutes. Drain, rinse well under cold running water, drain again and set aside.

2 Combine the onion, garlic and tomatoes in a food processor and process into a purée.

3 Heat the oil in a large frying pan or wok. Add the drained rice and sauté until it is golden brown. Using a slotted spoon, transfer the rice to a saucepan.

4 Reheat the oil remaining in the pan and cook the tomato purée for 2–3 minutes. Put it in the saucepan, pour in the stock and season to taste.

5 Bring to a boil, reduce the heat to the lowest setting, cover the pan and cook for 15–20 minutes, until almost all the liquid is absorbed. Slice the red chiles from tip to stem end into four or five sections. Place in a bowl of ice water until they curl back to form flowers, then drain.

6 Stir the peas into the rice mixture and cook, without a lid, until the liquid is absorbed and the rice tender. Stir the mixture occasionally.

7 Transfer the rice to a serving dish and garnish with the drained chile flowers and coriander sprigs. Warn your guests that these exotic chile "flowers" are hot and should be approached with caution.

Parsnip, Eggplant & Cashew Biryani

INGREDIENTS

1 small eggplant, sliced
3 onions
2 garlic cloves
1-inch piece of fresh ginger root, roughly chopped
3 tablespoons water
4 tablespoons corn oil
1½ cups unsalted cashews
¼ cup golden raisins
1 red bell pepper, seeded and sliced
3 parsnips, roughly chopped
1 teaspoon ground cumin
1 teaspoon ground coriander
½ teaspoon chili powder
½ cup plain yogurt
½ cup vegetable stock
1⅓ cups basmati rice, soaked
2 tablespoons butter
salt and ground black pepper
cilantro sprigs and quartered hard-boiled eggs,
to garnish

SERVES 4–6

1 Sprinkle the eggplant slices with salt and let drain for 30 minutes. Rinse the slices, pat dry and cut into bite-size pieces. Chop 1 onion roughly and place it in a food processor with the garlic and ginger. Add the water and process to a paste.

2 Slice the remaining onions finely. Heat 3 tablespoons of the oil in a pan and sauté the onions until golden. Drain well and place in a bowl. Stir-fry the cashews in the oil for 2 minutes, then add the golden raisins and fry until they swell. Using a slotted spoon, add to the onions in the bowl. Stir-fry the eggplant, bell pepper and parsnips for 5 minutes, then lift out with a slotted spoon and set aside.

3 Heat the remaining oil and cook the onion paste until golden. Stir in the spices and cook for 1 minute, then lower the heat and stir in the yogurt, stock and eggplant mixture. Bring to a boil, lower the heat and simmer for 30 minutes. Transfer the mixture to a baking dish and set aside.

4 Cook the drained rice in salted boiling water for 5 minutes, until tender but undercooked. Drain and mound on top of the vegetable mixture. Push a long spoon handle through the mixture and sprinkle the reserved onion mixture evenly on top. Dot with butter and cover with aluminum foil and a tight-fitting lid.

5 Bake the biryani for 35–40 minutes, then spoon onto a heated serving dish. Garnish with the fresh cilantro and hard-boiled eggs and serve.

Wild Rice with Broiled Vegetables

INGREDIENTS

scant ½ cup wild rice
⅔ cup long-grain rice
1 large eggplant, thickly sliced
1 each red, yellow and green bell peppers,
seeded and sliced
2 red onions, sliced
2 cups brown cap or shiitake mushrooms
2 small zucchini, cut in half lengthwise
olive oil, for brushing
2 tablespoons chopped fresh thyme
DRESSING
6 tablespoons extra virgin olive oil
2 tablespoons balsamic vinegar
2 garlic cloves, crushed
salt and ground black pepper

SERVES 4

2 Meanwhile, make the dressing. Mix the olive oil, vinegar and garlic in a screw-top jar. Add salt and pepper to taste, close the lid tightly and shake until thoroughly blended.

3 Arrange the eggplant, peppers, onions, mushroom and zucchini on a broiler pan. Brush with the olive oil and cook under a hot broiler for 8–10 minutes, until well browned. Turn the vegetables occasionally and brush with oil.

4 Drain the rice mixture and transfer it to a bowl. Shake the dressing again, pour half of it over the rice and mix. Spoon into a large serving dish and arrange the broiled vegetables on top. Drizzle on the remaining dressing and garnish with the thyme.

1 Put both types of rice in a pan of water and add salt. Bring to a boil, then lower the heat, cover and cook for 30–40 minutes or until the rice is tender.

COOK'S TIP
These vegetables taste and look wonderful when cooked on the grill. Use a solid ridged grill if you have one, to keep slices from falling onto the flame.

96

Persian Rice & Lentils

INGREDIENTS

2¼ cups basmati rice, soaked
⅔ cup oil
2 onions, 1 chopped and 1 thinly sliced
2 garlic cloves, crushed
⅔ cup green lentils, soaked and drained
2½ cups vegetable stock
⅓ cup raisins
2 teaspoons ground coriander
3 tablespoons tomato paste
1 egg yolk, beaten
2 teaspoons plain yogurt
6 tablespoons ghee, melted
few saffron threads soaked in
2 teaspoons boiling water
salt and ground black pepper
fresh herbs, to garnish

SERVES 8

1 Cook the drained rice in lightly salted boiling water for 3 minutes only. Drain well.

2 Heat 2 tablespoons of the oil in a deep saucepan and sauté the chopped onion and garlic for 5 minutes. Stir in the lentils, stock, raisins, coriander, tomato paste, and salt and pepper to taste. Bring to a boil, lower the heat, cover and simmer for 20 minutes.

3 Meanwhile, spoon 1 cup of the cooked rice into a bowl and stir in the egg yolk and yogurt. Add plenty of salt and pepper. Mix well.

4 Heat two-thirds of the remaining oil in a pan. Spread the yogurt-flavored rice on the bottom. Layer the plain rice and the lentil mixture in the pan, ending with the plain rice.

5 With a spoon handle, make three holes down to the bottom of the pan. Drizzle on the ghee. Turn the heat to high, then wrap the pan lid in a clean, wet dish towel and place on top. When steam appears, lower the heat and simmer for 30 minutes. Sauté the sliced onion until browned. Drain well.

6 Keeping the lid on, stand the pan of rice in cold water to loosen the golden crust on the bottom. Scoop about ¼ cup of the plain rice into a bowl, strain on the saffron water and mix lightly.

7 Toss the rice and lentil mixture and mound it on a platter. Sprinkle the saffron rice on top. Break up the rice crust on the bottom of the pan and place it around the mound. Sprinkle on the fried onion, garnish with fresh herbs and serve.

Nutty Rice & Mushroom Stir-fry

INGREDIENTS

3 tablespoons sunflower oil
4 cups cooked long-grain rice
1 small onion, roughly chopped
2 cups field mushrooms, sliced
½ cup hazelnuts,
roughly chopped
½ cup pecans, roughly chopped
½ cup blanched almonds,
roughly chopped
¼ cup chopped fresh parsley
salt and ground black pepper

SERVES 4–6

100

I Heat half the oil in a wok. Add the rice and stir-fry for 2–3 minutes over medium high heat. Remove the rice from the wok and set aside. Then heat the remaining  oil in the wok and stir-fry the chopped onion for 2 minutes, until softened.

2 Stir the sliced mushrooms into the wok with the onion. Toss over the heat for 2 more minutes.

3 Add all the nuts to the wok and stir-fry for 1 minute. Return the rice to the wok and stir-fry for 3 minutes. Add plenty of salt and pepper to taste. Stir in the chopped fresh parsley and serve immediately.

COOK'S TIP
This is a wonderful way of using up leftover rice. Try brown rice, as a variation, and add cashews instead of almonds.

Festive Rice

INGREDIENTS

2¼ cups Thai fragrant rice
¼ cup oil
2 garlic cloves, crushed
2 onions, finely sliced
2-inch piece of fresh turmeric,
peeled and crushed
3 cups water
1½ cups coconut milk
1–2 lemongrass stems, bruised
ACCOMPANIMENTS
omelet strips
2 fresh chiles, shredded
cucumber chunks
tomato wedges
deep-fried onions
shrimp crackers

SERVES 8

1 Wash the rice in several changes of water. Drain well. Heat the oil in a wok and gently sauté the garlic, onions and turmeric for 3–4 minutes, until the onions have softened but not browned.

2 Stir in the rice until coated, then pour in the water and coconut milk. Add the lemongrass. Bring to a boil, lower the heat and simmer for 15 minutes, until all the liquid has been absorbed.

3 Remove the pan from heat, cover with a clean dish towel and a tight-fitting lid and let stand in a warm place for 15 minutes.

4 Lift out the lemongrass and discard. Spread the rice mixture on a platter and garnish with the accompaniments. Serve immediately.

Green Lentil Filo Pie

Ingredients

*1 cup green lentils, soaked for
30 minutes in water to cover, drained
2 bay leaves
2 onions, sliced
5 cups chicken or vegetable stock
¾ cup butter, melted
1¼ cups long-grain rice,
preferably basmati
4 tablespoons chopped fresh parsley, plus
a few sprigs to garnish
2 tablespoons chopped fresh dill
1 egg, beaten
2 cups mushrooms, sliced
about 8 sheets filo pastry
3 eggs, hard-boiled and sliced
salt and ground black pepper*

Serves 6

102

1 Cover the lentils with water, then simmer with the bay leaves, one onion and half the stock for 20–25 minutes, or until tender. Season well. Set aside to cool.

2 Gently fry the remaining onion in another saucepan in 2 tablespoons of the butter, for 5 minutes. Stir in the rice and the rest of the stock. Season, bring to a boil, then cover and simmer for 12 minutes for basmati, 15 minutes for long grain. Let stand, uncovered, for 5 minutes, then stir in the fresh herbs and the beaten egg.

3 Fry the mushrooms in 3 tablespoons of the butter for 5 minutes, until they are just soft. Set aside to cool. Preheat the oven to 375°F.

4 Brush a large, shallow ovenproof dish with more butter. Lay the sheets of filo in it, covering the base but making sure most of the filo hangs over the sides. Brush the sheets of filo well with butter as you work, and overlap the pastry as required. Make sure there is a lot of pastry to fold over the green lentil filling.

5 Layer rice, lentils and mushrooms in the pastry shell, repeating the layers at least once and tucking the sliced egg in between. Season as you layer and form an even mound of filling. Bring up the sheets of pastry over the filling, scrunching the top into attractive folds. Brush all over with the rest of the butter and set aside to chill.

6 Bake the pie for about 45 minutes, until golden and crisp. Allow it to stand for 10 minutes before serving, garnished with parsley.

Tomato Rice

INGREDIENTS

2 tablespoons corn oil
½ teaspoon onion seeds
1 onion, sliced
2 tomatoes, sliced
1 orange or yellow bell pepper, seeded,
roughly chopped and cut into chunks
1 teaspoon grated fresh ginger root
1 garlic clove, crushed
1 teaspoon chili powder
2 tablespoons chopped cilantro
1 potato, diced
1½ teaspoons salt
scant ½ cup frozen peas
2 cups basmati rice, soaked
3 cups water

SERVES 4

2 Add the sliced tomatoes, pepper, ginger, garlic, chili powder, fresh cilantro, diced potato, salt and peas. Stir-fry over medium heat for 5 more minutes.

3 Stir in the drained rice until well coated. Pour in the water and bring to a boil, then lower the heat slightly, cover tightly and cook for 12–15 minutes. Remove the rice from heat, leaving the lid in place, and set aside for 5 minutes. Transfer to a warmed serving dish, stir the rice and serve.

1 Heat the oil in a large saucepan and sauté the onion seeds for about 30 seconds. Add the sliced onion and fry for 5 more minutes until they are lightly toasted.

Tofu Noodles

INGREDIENTS

8 ounces firm tofu
peanut oil, for deep-frying
6 ounces dried medium egg noodles
1 tablespoon sesame oil
1 teaspoon cornstarch
2 teaspoons dark soy sauce
2 tablespoons rice wine or dry sherry
1 teaspoon sugar
6–8 scallions, cut diagonally
into 1-inch lengths
3 garlic cloves, sliced
1 fresh green chili, seeded and sliced
4 ounces Chinese cabbage leaves,
coarsely shredded
2 ounces bean sprouts
½ cup cashews, toasted, to serve

SERVES 4

1 Drain the tofu, pat it dry with paper towels and cut into 1-inch cubes. Half-fill a wok with peanut oil and heat it to 350°F or until a cube of dried bread added to the oil browns in 30–45 seconds. Deep-fry the tofu in batches for 1–2 minutes or until golden brown. Drain on paper towels. Carefully pour all but 2 tablespoons of the oil from the wok.

2 Bring a saucepan of lightly salted water to a boil. Add the noodles and cook according to the instructions on the package. Drain, rinse under cold water and drain again. Transfer to a bowl and toss with 2 teaspoons of the sesame oil. Mix the cornstarch, soy sauce, rice wine, sugar and remaining sesame oil in a small bowl.

3 Reheat the oil in the wok and stir-fry the scallions, garlic, chili, Chinese cabbage and bean sprouts for 1–2 minutes. Toss in the tofu and noodles, then add the cornstarch mixture. Cook, stirring, for 1 minute. Sprinkle with the toasted cashews and serve.

Crispy Noodles with Mixed Vegetables

INGREDIENTS

2 large carrots
2 zucchini
4 scallions
4 ounces fine green beans
4 ounces dried rice vermicelli or
cellophane noodles
peanut oil, for deep-frying
1-inch piece of fresh ginger, peeled and cut into
shreds
1 fresh red chili, sliced
4 ounces fresh shiitake or button mushrooms,
thickly sliced
a few Chinese cabbage leaves, coarsely shredded
1½ cups bean sprouts
2 tablespoons light soy sauce
2 tablespoons rice wine or dry sherry
1 teaspoon sugar
2 tablespoons torn fresh cilantro leaves

SERVES 3–4

1 Cut the carrots, zucchini and scallions into matchsticks. Trim the beans. Break the vermicelli or noodles into 3-inch lengths.

2 Half-fill a wok with peanut oil and heat it to 350°F or until a cube of dried bread added to the oil browns in 30–45 seconds. Deep-fry the dried vermicelli, a handful at a time, for 1–2 minutes, until puffed up and crisp. Drain on paper towels. Carefully pour off all but 2 tablespoons of the oil from the wok.

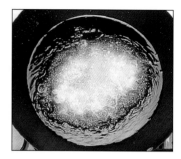

3 Reheat the oil in the wok and stir-fry the beans and carrots for 2–3 minutes. Add the ginger, chili, mushrooms and zucchini and stir-fry for 1–2 more minutes.

4 Add the Chinese cabbage, bean sprouts and scallions and stir-fry for 1 more minute. Spoon on the soy sauce, rice wine and sugar. Toss over the heat for 30 seconds, then add the vermicelli and the fresh cilantro. Toss to mix, taking care not to crush the noodles, then serve.

Sesame Noodle Salad with Hot Peanuts

INGREDIENTS

12 ounces dried egg noodles
2 carrots, cut into matchsticks
½ cucumber, peeled and cubed
4 ounces celery root, cut into matchsticks
6 scallions, finely sliced
8 canned water chestnuts, drained and finely sliced
1 cup bean sprouts
1 fresh green chili, seeded and finely chopped
2 tablespoons sesame seeds and
4 ounces peanuts, to serve

DRESSING

1 tablespoon dark soy sauce
1 tablespoon light soy sauce
1 tablespoon clear honey
1 tablespoon rice wine or dry sherry
1 tablespoon sesame oil

SERVES 4

108

1 Preheat the oven to 400°F. Bring a saucepan of lightly salted water to a boil. Add the noodles and cook according to the instructions on the package. Drain the noodles, rinse under cold water and drain again.

2 Transfer the noodles to a bowl and add the prepared vegetables, including the chili. Mix well. Combine the dressing ingredients in a small bowl, whisk lightly, then add to the salad and toss to coat. Divide the salad between four plates.

3 Spread out the sesame seeds and peanuts on separate baking sheets. Bake the sesame seeds for 5 minutes and the peanuts for 10 minutes or until evenly browned.

4 Sprinkle the roasted seeds and peanuts over the four plates of salad and serve.

Stir-fried Vegetables with Ribbon Noodles

INGREDIENTS

1 pound dried ribbon noodles,
such as tagliatelle
3 tablespoons corn oil
1/2-inch piece of fresh ginger, peeled
and finely chopped
2 garlic cloves, crushed
1 carrot, sliced diagonally
2 zucchini, quartered lengthwise,
then sliced diagonally
6 ounces wax beans, sliced diagonally
6 ounces baby corn cobs, halved lengthwise
6 tablespoons yellow bean sauce
6 scallions, sliced into 1-inch lengths
2 tablespoons rice wine or dry sherry
1 teaspoon sesame seeds
salt

SERVES 4

3 Stir in the yellow bean sauce. Toss over the heat for 2 minutes, then add the scallions, rice wine and drained ribbon noodles. Season with salt to taste. Toss over the heat for 1 minute to heat through. Sprinkle with the sesame seeds and serve immediately.

109

1 Bring a large saucepan of lightly salted water to a boil. Cook the ribbon noodles according to the instructions on the package. Drain, rinse under hot water and drain again. Transfer to a bowl and toss with 1 teaspoon of the oil.

2 Heat the rest of the oil in a wok or frying pan and stir-fry the ginger and garlic for 30 seconds, then add the vegetables. Stir-fry for 3–4 minutes.

Noodles with Shiitake & Red Onion

Ingredients

1¼ pounds thin dried tagliarini
3 tablespoons sesame oil
1 red onion, thinly sliced
4 ounces fresh shiitake mushrooms, trimmed
and thinly sliced
3 tablespoons dark soy sauce
1 tablespoon balsamic vinegar
2 teaspoons superfine sugar
1 teaspoon salt
celery leaves, to garnish

Serves 6

110

3 Add the noodles to the wok, with the soy sauce, balsamic vinegar, superfine sugar and salt. Stir-fry for 1 more minute, then add the remaining sesame oil. Toss over the heat for 30 seconds. Garnish with celery leaves and serve immediately.

1 Bring a large saucepan of lightly salted water to a boil. Add the noodles and cook according to the instructions on the package. Drain, rinse under hot water and drain again. Transfer into a bowl and toss with 1 teaspoon of the oil.

2 Meanwhile, heat a wok, add 1 tablespoon of the remaining oil and stir-fry the onion and shiitake mushrooms for 2 minutes.

Zucchini with Noodle Needles

INGREDIENTS

1 pound zucchini
2 tablespoons vegetable oil
1 onion, thinly sliced
1 garlic clove, crushed
½ teaspoon ground turmeric
2 tomatoes, chopped
3 tablespoons water
14 ounces cooked shrimp, peeled and deveined
1 ounce cellophane noodles
salt or soy sauce

SERVES 4–6

I Use a vegetable peeler to cut thin strips from the outside of each zucchini. Cut the zucchini into thin slices. The slices will have decorative edges.

2 Heat the oil in a frying pan or wok and fry the onion and garlic for 5 minutes, until softened but not browned. Stir in the zucchini slices and ground turmeric, then add the chopped tomatoes, water and shrimp.

3 Put the noodles in a saucepan and pour boiling water over them to cover. Set aside for 1–2 minutes, then drain. Snip into 2- inch "needles" and add to the vegetables.

4 Cover with a lid and cook the noodles and vegetables in their own steam for 2–3 minutes. Toss well, season to taste with salt or soy sauce and serve immediately.

Thai Noodle Salad

INGREDIENTS

12 ounces dried somen noodles
1 large carrot, cut into thin strips
1 bunch asparagus, trimmed and cut into
1½-inch lengths
4 ounces snow peas, trimmed and halved
4 ounces baby corn cobs, halved lengthwise
1 red bell pepper, seeded and cut into fine strips
2 cups bean sprouts
8 canned water chestnuts, drained and
thinly sliced
lime wedges, chopped roasted peanuts and
fresh cilantro leaves, to garnish

DRESSING

3 tablespoons torn fresh basil leaves
5 tablespoons roughly chopped mint leaves
2 scallions, thinly sliced
1 tablespoon grated fresh ginger
2 garlic cloves, crushed
1 cup coconut milk
2 tablespoons dark sesame oil
juice of 1 lime
salt and cayenne pepper

SERVES 4–6

1 Make the dressing. Combine the fresh herbs and scallions in a bowl. Add the ginger and garlic, coconut milk, sesame oil and lime juice. Whisk well, then season to taste with the salt and cayenne.

2 Bring a saucepan of lightly salted water to a boil. Add the noodles and cook according to the instructions on the package. Drain, rinse under cold water and drain again.

3 Cook the carrot, asparagus, snow peas and corn in separate saucepans of lightly salted boiling water until crisptender. Drain, refresh under cold water and drain again. Transfer to a bowl and add the red pepper, bean sprouts and water chestnuts.

4 Add the noodles and dressing to the bowl and toss well. Arrange on individual plates and garnish with the lime wedges, peanuts and cilantro leaves.

112

Fruit & Vegetable Gado-Gado

INGREDIENTS

½ cucumber, sliced
2 pears, not too ripe
1–2 apples
2 tablespoons lemon juice
1 head crisp lettuce, shredded
6 small tomatoes, cut into wedges
3 fresh pineapple slices, cored and
cut into wedges
12 hard-cooked quail's eggs, shelled
6 ounces dried egg noodles, cooked, rinsed,
drained and cut into short lengths
salt
deep-fried onions, to garnish
PEANUT SAUCE
1 tablespoon sambal oelek or chili sauce
1¼ cups coconut milk
1 cup crunchy peanut butter
1 tablespoon dark soy sauce
2 teaspoons thick tamarind water
1 tablespoon peanuts, coarsely crushed
salt

SERVES 6

1 Put the cucumber slices in a colander and sprinkle them with salt. Let sit in the sink for 15 minutes to drain, then rinse thoroughly and drain again.

2 Then make the peanut sauce. Mix the sambal oelek with the coconut milk in a saucepan. Add the peanut butter and heat gently, stirring, until the sauce is smooth and thick. Stir in the soy sauce and tamarind water. Pour the sauce into a bowl and sprinkle with the crushed peanuts to serve.

3 Peel the pears and the apples, remove the cores and slice thinly into a bowl. Toss with the lemon juice. Arrange the fruit slices on a platter with the lettuce wedges, cucumber slices, tomatoes and pineapple wedges.

4 Arrange the quail's eggs over the salad and add the chopped noodles and deep-fried onions. Serve with the peanut sauce.

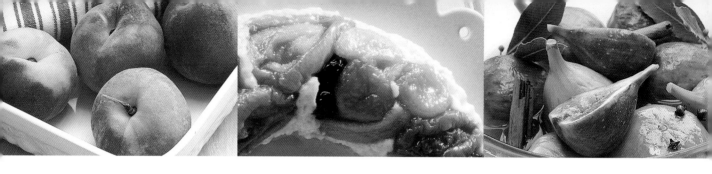

DESSERTS

Caramel Rice Pudding

INGREDIENTS

5 tablespoons short-grain pudding rice
5 tablespoons sugar
14-ounce can evaporated milk,
made up to 2½ cups with water
pat of butter
2 apples
1 small fresh pineapple
2 teaspoons lemon juice

SERVES 4

118

1 Preheat the oven to 300°F. Lightly grease a soufflé dish. Put the rice in a sieve and wash thoroughly under cold water. Drain well and transfer to the soufflé dish.

2 Add 2 tablespoons of the sugar to the dish. Pour in the diluted evaporated milk and stir. Dot the surface with butter. Bake for 2 hours, then let cool for 30 minutes.

3 Meanwhile, core and slice the apples. Peel and core the pineapple and cut it into chunks. Put the fruit in a bowl. Add the lemon juice and toss lightly. Preheat the broiler to high.

4 Sprinkle the remaining sugar onto the baked pudding. Broil until the sugar has caramelized. Let stand for 5 minutes, to let the caramel topping harden, then serve with the fresh fruit.

Souffléed Rice Pudding

INGREDIENTS

5 tablespoons short-grain pudding rice, rinsed
3 tablespoons honey
3 cups milk
½ teaspoon vanilla extract
2 egg whites
1 teaspoon grated nutmeg

SERVES 4

3 Whisk the egg whites in a clean, dry bowl until soft peaks form. Using a large metal spoon, fold them lightly and evenly into the rice mixture. Transfer the

mixture to the prepared dish and level the surface.

4 Sprinkle with grated nutmeg and bake for 15–20 minutes, until the pudding is well risen and golden brown. Serve hot.

119

1 Place the rice, honey and milk in a heavy saucepan. Bring to just below the boiling point, then simmer over the lowest possible heat for 1–1¼ hours, stirring occasionally, until most of the liquid has been absorbed.

2 Preheat the oven to 425°F. Lightly grease a 4-cup ovenproof dish. Away from the heat, stir the vanilla extract into the rice mixture and set the saucepan aside to cool slightly.

Moroccan Rice Pudding

INGREDIENTS

¼ cup blanched almonds, chopped
1¾ cups very hot water
¾ cup short-grain pudding rice,
rinsed
2 tablespoons butter
3-inch piece of cinnamon stick
pinch of salt
½ teaspoon almond extract
14-ounce can condensed milk,
made up to 2½ cups with
low-fat milk
2 tablespoons orange flower water
toasted sliced almonds and ground cinnamon,
to decorate

SERVES 6

120

1 Process the almonds in a blender or food processor until very fine, then add ½ cup of the hot water and process again. Strain through a sieve into a large saucepan, pressing the nut pulp against the mesh with a spoon to extract as much liquid as possible.

2 Stir the remaining hot water into the almond "milk" and bring to a boil. Add the rice and half the butter to the pan, then add the cinnamon stick. Stir in the salt and almond extract. Pour in half the diluted condensed milk mixture and stir well.

3 Bring to a boil, stirring constantly, then simmer over the lowest possible heat for 1–1½ hours, stirring in the remaining milk mixture toward the end of the cooking time, until the pudding is thick and creamy. Stir in the orange flower water.

4 Pour the rice pudding into a warmed serving bowl, sprinkle with the sliced almonds and dot with the remaining butter. Dust the ground cinnamon on top and serve.

COOK'S TIP
This is delicious with a topping of plain yogurt and a drizzle of honey. Use a delicately scented honey, such as orange blossom.

Fruited Rice Ring

INGREDIENTS

5 tablespoons short-grain pudding rice,
rinsed
3¾ cups milk
2-inch piece of cinnamon stick
1 cup dried fruit mix
¾ cup orange juice
oil, for brushing
3 tablespoons sugar
thinly grated zest of 1 small orange
whipped cream, to serve (optional)

SERVES 4

I Place the rice, milk and cinnamon stick in a large saucepan. Bring to a boil, then simmer over the lowest possible heat for about 1½ hours, stirring occasionally, until all the liquid has been absorbed.

2 Meanwhile, mix the dried fruit and orange juice in a second pan. Bring to a boil, lower the heat, cover and simmer for about 1 hour, until the fruit is tender and no liquid remains. Brush a 6-cup ring mold lightly with oil.

3 Remove the cinnamon stick from the rice. Gently stir in the sugar and grated orange zest. Spread out the fruit on the bottom of the ring pan. Spoon in the rice, smoothing it down firmly. Cover with plastic wrap and chill for 3–4 hours.

4 Run a knife around the rim of the mold to loosen the rice ring. Invert a serving dish on top and carefully turn over both mold and plate. Serve with a spoonful of whipped cream, if desired.

Rice Sundae

INGREDIENTS

¼ cup short-grain pudding rice
2½ cups milk
1 teaspoon vanilla extract
½ teaspoon ground cinnamon
3 tablespoons sugar
TO SERVE
raspberries, strawberries or blueberries,
thawed if frozen
chocolate sauce and toasted sliced almonds
(optional)

SERVES 4

1 Put the rice, and milk, vanilla extract, cinnamon and sugar into a saucepan. Bring to a boil, stirring constantly, then lower the heat and simmer for

30–40 minutes, stirring occasionally and adding more milk if needed, until the grains are soft.

2 Spoon the mixture into a bowl and set aside to cool, stirring occasionally to prevent a skin from forming. When cold, chill the mixture in the refrigerator

3 Just before serving, stir the mixture well. Spoon it into four sundae dishes. Top with raspberries, strawberries or blueberries and add the chocolate sauce and toasted sliced almonds, if using.

COOK'S TIP

Rice puddings are wonderfully versatile.
Try this with dates or apricots stewed in a syrup
flavored with rosewater. For a very rich pudding,
use half milk and half cream; for a lighter dish,
use skim milk and top with fresh fruit
and plain yogurt.

Thai Rice Cake

INGREDIENTS

*generous 1 cup Thai fragrant rice or
jasmine rice*
4 cups milk
½ cup sugar
6 cardamom pods, cracked open
2 bay leaves
1¼ cups whipping cream
6 eggs, separated
TOPPING
1¼ cups heavy cream
scant 1 cup low-fat cream cheese, softened
1 teaspoon vanilla extract
grated zest of 1 lemon
3 tablespoons sugar
*soft berries and sliced star fruit and kiwi,
to decorate*

SERVES 8–10

1 Grease and line the bottom of a deep 10-inch round cake pan. Bring a large saucepan of unsalted water to a boil and cook the rice for 3 minutes. Drain the rice thoroughly.

2 Return the rice to the pan. Add the milk, sugar, cracked cardamoms and bay leaves. Bring to a boil, then lower the heat and simmer for 20 minutes, stirring occasionally. Transfer the mixture to a bowl and set it aside to cool.

3 Remove the bay leaves and cardamom husks from the mixture. Beat in the whipping cream, then the egg yolks. Preheat the oven to 350°F.

4 Whisk the egg whites in a clean, dry bowl until soft peaks form. Fold into the rice mixture. Spoon into the prepared pan and bake for 45–50 minutes, until risen and golden brown. The center should be slightly soft—it will firm up as it cools.

5 Chill the cooked rice cake overnight in the pan, then turn out onto a large serving plate. Whip the heavy cream until stiff, then mix with the cream cheese, vanilla extract, lemon zest and sugar.

6 Cover the top and sides of the cake with the cream mixture, swirling it attractively. Decorate with the soft berries and the sliced star fruit and kiwi.

Mangoes with Sticky Rice

INGREDIENTS

generous ½ cup white glutinous (sticky) rice
¾ cup thick coconut milk
3 tablespoons sugar
pinch of salt
2 ripe mangoes
strips of pared lime zest, to decorate

SERVES 4

126

1 Rinse the glutinous rice thoroughly in several changes of cold water. Let soak overnight in a bowl of fresh, cold water.

2 Drain the rice and spread it in an even layer in a steamer lined with muslin or cheese-cloth. Cover and steam for about 20 minutes or until the grains are tender.

3 Meanwhile, skim off 3 tablespoons from the top of the coconut milk and set it aside. Heat the remaining coconut milk with the sugar and salt in a saucepan. Stir until the sugar dissolves, then bring to a boil. Pour into a bowl and cool slightly.

4 Transfer the rice to a bowl and pour in the sweetened coconut milk. Stir well, let stand for 10–15 minutes so that the rice absorbs some of the liquid, then spoon into a serving dish.

5 Peel the mangoes and slice the flesh thinly. Arrange the fruit on top of the rice pudding and drizzle on the reserved coconut milk. Decorate the pudding with strips of lime zest.

Index